What Matters?

Dedication

To our friend and colleague Richard Maltby, without whose guidance, support, wisdom and fellowship this book would have been inconceivable.

WHAT MATTERS?

Talking Value in Australian Culture

Julian Meyrick, Robert Phiddian and Tully Barnett

MONASH University Publishing

Monash University Publishing
Matheson Library and Information Services Building
40 Exhibition Walk
Monash University
Clayton, Victoria 3800, Australia
www.publishing.monash.edu

Monash University Publishing brings to the world publications which advance the best traditions of humane and enlightened thought.

Monash University Publishing titles pass through a rigorous process of independent peer review.

ISBN: 9781925523805 (paperback)
ISBN: 9781925523829 (PDF)
ISBN: 9781925523812 (ePub)

www.publishing.monash.edu/books/wm-9781925523805.html

Series: Cultural Studies

Design: Les Thomas

Front cover image: Jon Kudelka "Artonomics", first published in *The Australian*, 8 October 2016

A catalogue record for this book is available from the National Library of Australia

Printed in Australia by Griffin Press an Accredited ISO AS/NZS 14001:2004 Environmental Management System printer.

Contents

Acknowledgments

The Laboratory Adelaide: The Value of Culture project was funded by the Australian Research Council (LP140100802) and our partners the State Library of South Australia, the State Theatre Company of South Australia, and the Adelaide Festival.

Thank you to our collaborators on this project: Professor Steve Brown, Professor Richard Maltby, Heather Robinson, Dr Fiona Sprott and Matt Russell.

And to the cultural institutions that gave up their time to talk to us.

Introduction

When Did Culture Become a Number?

'The demand for certainty is one which is natural to man, but
is nevertheless an intellectual vice … To endure uncertainty
is difficult, but so are most of the other virtues.'

Bertrand Russell

When did culture become a number? When did the books, paintings, poems, plays, songs, films, games, art installations, clothes, and all the myriad objects that fill our lives and which we consider cultural, become a matter of statistical measurement? When did the *value* of culture become solely a matter of the quantifiable *benefits* it provides, and the latter become subject to input–output analysis in what government budgets refer to as 'the cultural function'? When did experience become data?

Perhaps a more important question is why did it happen, and why does it keep happening? Also, how does it happen? Culture is innate to being human. Thick books have been written describing culture's myriad expressions and meanings. Culture has been around for as long as humanity itself. And the question of its value is not new. We cannot claim the modern world is answering it exclusively. But why are we answering it in the way that we are – by turning it into something to be scaled, measured and benchmarked? Who loses and who gains?

These are big questions of more than academic or Australian import. They are, indeed, much broader than arts and culture, as a recent crop of studies describing the unintended effects of the rise of 'metric power' suggests.[1] So this modest book based on local experiences will nevertheless be of interest beyond Australia and the usual suspects of the cultural debate. Our core contention is that datafied modes of analysis are claiming authority over domains of human existence they have limited capacity for understanding. If you are researching an influenza epidemic, more data is better data. If you are studying Australian film, more data is informative but not definitive because questions of artistic merit can only be judged. If you are assessing Christina Stead's *The Man Who Loved Children*, massified data is close to useless. At a time when even accountants are looking for a more compelling understanding of value,[2] it is imperative that the arts – a domain where individual experience is central – resist the evangelical call of quantification, and winnow its potential benefit from its real and deleterious risks.

This book addresses anyone seriously interested in the value of arts and culture. It particularly addresses those with an operational interest: arts practitioners, managers of cultural organisations, policy makers, leaders of cultural programs at all levels of government, philanthropists and board members, critics (within and outside the academy) and so on. We hope to influence public debate about the value of culture, to encourage people to see their cultural experiences in that debate, and not feel some strange urge to 'speak the 'language of government'. This can be extremely alienating. Consider a 2008 Australian Bureau of Statistics paper, *Towards Comparable Statistics for Cultural Heritage Organisations*. It proposes 'a list of Key Measures ... balancing the priority of items across four

---

1   See especially David Beer, *Metric Power* (London: Palgrave Macmillan, 2016); and also Jerry Z. Muller, *The Tyranny of Metrics* (Princeton: Princeton University Press, 2018); Cathy O'Neil, *Weapons of Math Destruction: How Big Data Increases Inequality and Threatens Democracy* (New York: Crown, 2016); and Stefan Collini, *Speaking of Universities* (London; New York: Verso, 2017).

2   See Jane Gleeson-White, *Six Capitals: The Revolution Capitalism has to Have; or, Can Accountants Save the Planet?* (New York: WW Norton & Company, 2015).

cultural heritage domains with the feasibility of producing standard guidelines for collecting data'.[3] The five Key Measures it puts forward – Attendance, Visitor Characteristics, Financial Resources, Human Resources and The Collection – subsume 18 Detailed Measures, with a list of Counting Rules for each: 'There are eleven different counting methods required to count the variety of items held in the collections … These eleven groups of items are designed to cover all the items held across cultural heritage organisations'.

This is a long way from browsing a library shelf, or walking through an exhibition. A long way from reading a book, contemplating the mystery of ancient artefacts, or librarians helping people navigate online genealogy portals. Such language generates a world of arithmetical marks, and the sums and inferences considered legitimate to those marks. Where does the *experience* of going to a library or museum fit in? Not in ABS statistics, obviously, and no doubt the Bureau would not think itself competent to pronounce on such 'qualitative' matters. Who does then? And how do 'qualitative' matters sit with quantitative enumeration (which always seems more precise, if only because that's how numbers look)?

These are important questions. The datafication of arts and culture is only a few decades old, so it is not an essential or inevitable element of their assessment. What happens when this is the major way we describe their place in our lives? In 2013, we began a university research project of moderate scope seeking to understand how quantitative and qualitative indicators align in government measures of culture. As we were in Adelaide, we made that city our focus. We called the project Laboratory Adelaide because we saw it as a case study with a rich cultural history and an active contemporary arts scene: a petri dish of just the right scale.

---

3   *ABS "Information Paper: Towards Comparable Statistics for Cultural Heritage Organisations" 4916.0, 2008: 37.*

To get our research off the ground, we held a lunch for some of Adelaide's cultural leaders. Over dessert, we asked them what they wanted us to achieve. The answer was instructive: a way to talk truthfully about what they do. They were, they said, unable to incorporate their real motivations and experiences into their reporting. Could we find a new, better way of communicating the actual value of arts and culture?

For the first year this seemed a simple enough goal. After all, these people were doing things the public had ready access to. Both state and local government in South Australia had a record of acknowledging the contribution of culture. They supported a range of cultural organisations and events – especially festivals, which are a big part of Adelaide's civic life. There was a sense that everyone already knew how important culture was to the state. But when it came to *demonstrating* its value, the words weren't there. Our job was to fix that. As humanities scholars, we felt we were in a good position to do so. After all, didn't we spend our lives talking about culture?

As the second year drew on, a note of uncertainty entered the project. By now we were starting to publish, and articulate in a series of articles, columns, notes, letters and emails, the dimensions of the problem as we saw it – the short time-scales governments deploy to evaluate outcomes, for example, which ignore culture's longer-term contribution. Or the woolly use of language in policy documents, that makes the precise meaning of terms like 'excellence' and 'innovation' impossible to pin down. These issues, and others, have serious assessment implications. But it goes beyond this, highlighting a basic misapprehension of culture by governments, not on a human level – politicians and policy makers, like the rest of us, read books, watch films and listen to music – but on the official level. Their grasp of culture may be a sure one, personally. But when it comes to acknowledging that value publically, government measurement strategies, like those of Adelaide's cultural leaders, seem to fall forever short of the requisite level of proof.

Meanwhile, political events intervened and the Australian cultural sector exploded like a supernova. In 2015, the then federal Arts Minister, George Brandis, raided the budget of the federal arts agency, the Australia Council of the Arts, to set up his own, personally administered grant body. To say this came as a shock to arts practitioners would be a considerable understatement. The minister's actions contradicted 30 years of cross-party consensus about how culture in Australia should be federally funded – via independent agencies – and rendered his support of the Council's 2014–19 Strategic Plan a sham. The sector went into uproar. Where did the years of accumulated data on the demonstrable benefits of arts and culture figure in this fiery clash of ideologies?

The answer is that they didn't. The numerical proofs of culture's value (mainly economic value) that have been cascading through government consciousness since the 1970s were nowhere to be seen (see Box 1: The Funding Game). Below, we give a description of what *was* involved, but for Laboratory Adelaide it confirmed a sinking feeling: the problem of the value of culture is not a methodological one. It cannot be addressed by a new metric or a different categorical disaggregation. Use of measurement indicators assumes a degree of background understanding that too often isn't there at a policy level. The quantitative demonstrations of value we were trying to improve don't make sense for culture. They flatten out its history, purpose and meaning.

This realisation put us at odds with expert views (see Chapter 5 'On the Importance of Not Being an Expert') about the role of culture in post-industrial societies today. These views are typically upbeat about culture's economic and urban 'vibrancy'. Charles Landry's 'creative cities', Richard Florida's 'creative class', John Hartley and Terry Flew's 'creative industries' – the ideas of these authors, and others of similar ilk, are practical and positive (though Florida has recently retreated to a gloomier position).[4] The 'creative industries' approach, for example, treats policy-making processes with a benign eye and admits no serious difficulties when it comes to proving the benefits culture provides. This chipper outlook is mirrored by swarms of local efforts around Australia today to develop bespoke systems of 'cultural indicators', each slightly different, yet each beholden to the same underlying assumption: that the value of culture can be numerically demonstrated.

By now we were participating in specialised symposia and conferences, and consulting broadly among arts agencies and peak bodies. There are 537 local councils in Australia, six states, two territories and one federal government. It sometimes seemed to us they were all looking for the perfect metric. We sat through presentation after presentation on quantitative approaches to culture's value. At the end, hands would invariably go up and people say they were developing a 'similar measurement model'.

Yet underneath the relentless optimism, we sensed a current of troubled preoccupation. It went by different names: 'the intrinsic value of culture', 'the inherent value of culture', '(the) cultural value (of culture)'. In this dry form it seems just another dimension of culture's value, to be arraigned alongside the others: its economic value, its social value, its heritage value, etc. It is not. It is code for all that is left *out* of measurement indices, which is to say our whole *sense* of culture, of what culture *means*. It seems obvious to say it, but in culture No Meaning = No Value. It may not be true of boots, bread and billiard balls. But it is absolutely true of symbolic goods like paintings, performances and books.

---

4   See Richard Florida, *The New Urban Crisis: How Our Cities Are Increasing Inequality, Deepening Segregation, and Failing the Middle Class – and What We Can Do about It* (New York: Basic Books, 2017).

For thousands, possibly tens of thousands of years, culture has been supported through patronage. Whether it came from kings, popes or rich merchants, it came the same way: by someone seeing a particular cultural thing or activity and personally choosing to fund it. We have replaced this simple, if limited, support mechanism with distanced assessment processes of Heath-Robinson complexity. These processes – involving submission forms, acquittal procedures, classification systems, priority lists – introduce a loss of fidelity to the immediacy of cultural experience. They are generalised and abstract, with cultural experience therefore framed as a matter of personal taste, and opinions in relation to it 'subjective'. Numbers present as 'objective', whether or not they reflect the core elements of culture. Hence the desire to quantify as much of its assessment as possible.

Even the best set of numbers never stops governments for long, though. Like the mirages of water on a hot road that disappear as you draw close to them, the pursuit of numbers begets only the pursuit of more numbers. You might count, for example, the number of people going to a music concert (a measure of frequency). But did they have a good time (the value proposition)? You might question some of them, and rank their answers (on a preference scale of 1 to 5). But were they being truthful (response bias)? You might look for changes in their market choices thereafter (acquisition of consumption skills). But what of less obvious effects – on wellbeing, level of education, social participation, civic cohesion? More indices, more numbers. The search for certainty produces ever-more uncertain measures, each a further step away from the actual experience of culture. As the numbers get more rubbery and elaborate, people's trust in them diminishes.

And it's expensive. The statistical habit, like any habit, is one that requires significant investment. Is there a cost–benefit analysis to be done on our obsession with cost–benefit analysis? Should a major theatre company, for example, outsource its costume department to spend the savings on an in-house metrics dashboard? At what point do we stop trying to measure something and try to understand it better? What would this involve, exactly, if we were to do it?

And it doesn't help. The ever more elaborate datafication of culture hasn't secured more money for arts and culture in Australia, or distributed the extant money better. If it assists an organisation to obtain an increase in public support in one grant round, there is no guarantee it will continue in the next.

This was the problem of culture's value as it appeared to us in our third year, when we saw the full extent of what we had stumbled into. Beneath the inexorable pursuit of numbers-driven data lay a Dante-esque vortex of hope, despair, panic and bewilderment masked by the neutral patois of quantitative analysis – the bullshit language that Adelaide's cultural leaders resented so deeply. In contemporary assessment processes, many arguments can be advanced for culture's value, but culture itself is not an argument. It is like asking someone to justify transport but forbidding any mention of cars. The bullshit has to be all about fuel sales, industrial development and urban expansion.

So where to from here? It is a question with profound implications, and not one Laboratory Adelaide can answer conclusively. However, we have identified some of the difficulties in valuing culture that governments and the public must meet head-on. They are not the only problems, but they are important ones:

1. The fact that assessment processes claim to measure value but leave *out* the human experience of culture, and turn it into a set of abstract, categorical traits.

2. The fact that assessment processes are preoccupied with short-term effects, ignore the longer-term trajectories of

cultural projects, and have a sense of history that is flat and inorganic.

3. The fact that assessment processes use language and phrases empty of specific meaning for culture (i.e. bullshit), or valorise words that have no universally agreed definition.

4. The fact that the people who experience culture are treated as consumers in a marketplace rather than members of a public, so public value (the underlying purpose of public investment) is inadequately addressed.

5. The fact that cultural organisations are regarded as scaled-up delivery mechanisms for policy outcomes, rather than as a serious and nuanced ecology worthy of study and support.

6. The fact that too often the value of culture comes down to its monetary value, directly and indirectly.

These problems interpenetrate. Evaluation strategies aren't grounded in cultural experience, so the language of official assessment is fuzzy and dead. Participants in culture are treated as consumers rather than citizens, so a flat-earth econometric idea of time becomes paramount, with its diminished conception of investment and return. *Ergo* cultural organisations are seen as platforms rather than as historical entities interlocked in rich and important relationships. *Ergo* culture's monetary value prevails over all other kinds of value – which in turn displaces cultural experience from the fulcrum of assessment, and encourages its breakdown into supposedly quantifiable 'benefits'.

At this point, those objecting to our opinions might say 'What's wrong with wanting to know what the public dollars invested in culture produce by way of economic and social outcomes?' The instrumental view of culture has its supporters, but our argument is not that culture's external impacts are being put above its internal qualities. Rather, it is being treated as a *function*. You can take an instrumental view of culture and still credit culture's specific nature and needs. But once it is turned into a function it collapses into a series of effects, and evaluation strategies become no more than the management of those effects. This isn't throwing the baby out with the bathwater. It's blowing up the bathroom. Functionalism rules so completely that culture isn't considered in any meaningful way at all.

Objectors might then say that culture *is* considered in assessment processes, by way of peer review and ministerial oversight. They are right to some extent – but it is a declining extent. Peer assessors and politicians retain an important role in how culture is evaluated in Australia today, both before and after it attracts government funding. But compared to the huge social outlay in gathering statistics and developing metrics, our almost religious faith in quantitative measurement, the place of *judgment* in valuing culture is a reluctant admission, an ageing relative inclined to embarrassing assertions, to be kept on a tight statistical leash. There is no ABS handbook 'On Peer Evaluation in Cultural Assessment Processes', still less one called 'Towards Appointing a Successful Arts Minister'. The human dimension of the problem of value is presumed to take care of itself. Only when it goes wrong, as it did under Senator Brandis, does it become a matter of strong attention.

In 2008, Brian McMaster, in a report for the UK's Department of Culture, Media & Sport, laid out a different framework for assessing culture, one that

> depends upon the funding bodies having the confidence and authority to make judgements that are respected by the arts community … As part of this new framework …

funding bodies will need to lay out clear expectations of
what they expect in return for their funding and what they
will be assessing and reporting to the Government and the
public ... Evidence would be based on the self-assessments
provided by cultural organisations and supplemented by the
peer review and funders' dialogue with the organisations.
In this context funders would recognise that not all risks
will be successful and that failure should not necessarily be
penalised. The quid pro quo for getting rid of cumbersome
targets, however, must be an understanding and acceptance
that there needs to be dialogue between funders and
organisations on the issues of excellence, innovation and
risk-taking.[5]

Supporting Excellence in the Arts: Fom Measurement to Judgement is
not a soft-headed document. It recognises that arts and culture
today must fulfil an array of social expectations if they want to
attract public money and political support. The difference between
McMaster and the ABS is that the former recognises that judgment
is central to assessing value, while the latter is fixated on counting
traits. There is nothing wrong with counting. Counting is an
important measurement tool. It is when counting takes the place
of judgment that evaluation goes awry. Under these circumstances,
the reality of culture parts company from official ideas of it, ideas
that circulate in an abstract policy realm without touching the
lived experience of people. This is not supportable for long, and
eventually something will give, occasionally in spectacular fashion.
In 2015, there was an example of just this in Australian cultural
policy.

---

5   Brian McMaster, *Supporting Excellence in the Arts: From Measurement to Judgement* (London: Department for Culture, Media and Sport, 2008), 23.

The Trouble with George

In March 2013, Julia Gillard's Labor government handed down its long-awaited national cultural policy, *Creative Australia*.[6] Delayed year after year because extra funding couldn't be found to support it or because the government had bigger fish to fry, the policy was finally released just before a federal election. The new Liberal government unceremoniously binned it within months of coming to power. Around this time Laboratory Adelaide had a meeting with some federal arts bureaucrats and were told 'we don't mention *Creative Australia* any more'. Six years of research and industry consultation were suddenly off the table.

George Brandis, who had been a vocal critic of the Australia Council at the time of the amending of its legislation in 2012, became Australia's new federal Arts Minister. Thus began a fractious time for culture that saw angry outbursts from the minister, harsh budget cuts from the government, an upsurge of protest from artists, and eventually a Senate Inquiry that attracted 2,719 submissions. What happened under Senator Brandis was unprecedented and unprecedentedly painful. But from the perspective of Laboratory Adelaide it brilliantly illuminated the problems Australia has with valuing culture. Don't waste a good crisis, as the saying goes. So what happened exactly?

It is important to note that Brandis's appointment as Arts Minister was at first welcomed. As a small 'l' Alfred Deakin-style Liberal with a keen interest in the arts – in music and literature especially – the general perception was that here, at last, was a politician who actually knew something about culture; he had a double degree in Arts and Law after all. Brandis's tone in the run-up to the election

---

6   See Julian Meyrick, 'Assemblage of Convenience: National Cultural Policy-making 101', *Australian Book Review*, May 2013, 12–14.

was measured and thoughtful. And his defence of culture *qua* culture was robust:

> Brandis says his differences with Labor are philosophical: arts policy should recognise and promote intrinsic values – art for art's sake – and not treat culture as a tool for other policy goals … 'The moment you embrace a derivative view – that we fund the arts because they are an aspect of telecommunications policy, or they're an aspect of education policy, or they're an aspect of trade policy – I think you both devalue the importance of cultural policy in its own right, and you demean the arts as one of the great human activities. But also in a practical sense you make the arts mendicant because they depend on the policy priorities of other, usually more powerful, departments of government.'[7]

For most arts ministers the first months in office are unsteady ones when they must rapidly come to terms with a diverse and feisty sector. Thereafter things go more smoothly. For Senator Brandis it was the other way round. At first, there were lots of photographs of the minister enjoying arts occasions, often in the company of Julie Bishop, the Foreign Minister, indicating a policy approach inflected by a cultural diplomacy agenda, but still a positive one. Then, in February 2014, nearly a year after his taking office, artists working with the Biennale of Sydney protested at its links with Transfield Services Ltd. The Biennale's Chair, Luca Belgiorno-Nettis, was a wealthy philanthropist and a long-time supporter of the cultural event. Transfield Services Ltd, who built and serviced offshore detention centres for Australia's marine-arriving asylum seekers, were part-owned by Transfield Holdings, Belgiorno-Nettis's family firm. A letter of objection signed by 46 artists led

---

7   Matthew Westwood, 'George Brandis details Coalition's arts manifesto', *The Australian*, 20 August 2013.

to nine withdrawing from the upcoming exhibition, which in turn forced Belgiorno-Nettis to resign. Brandis was furious. He wrote to the Australia Council, funders of the Biennale, demanding it exclude those refusing corporate sponsorship for political reasons – the first time an Australian arts minister has condemned artists for *not* taking money. He fumed,

> Artists like everybody else are entitled to voice their
> political opinions but I view with deep concern the effective
> blackballing of a benefactor, implicit in this decision,
> merely because of its commercial arrangements. Even more
> damagingly, the decision sends precisely the wrong message
> to other actual or potential corporate sponsors of the arts:
> that they may be insulted, and possibly suffer reputational
> damage, if an arts company or festival decides to make
> a political statement about an aspect of their commercial
> relationships with government, where it disapproves of
> a particular government policy which those commercial
> relationships serve.[8]

Darkly, the minister warned that the Biennale's Australia Council grant was soon up for renewal and he had 'no doubt that the decision about it will have regard to [this] episode and the damage it has done'. However, when the federal Budget was delivered in May, culture was not singled out for punitive treatment. Certainly, its allocation was reduced, but this was true of other areas of government expenditure. In winter 2014, the Australia Council launched a new Strategic Plan with mild fanfare at the Sydney Opera House. Brandis stood on the podium, seemingly supportive,

---

8   Letter from Senator George Brandis to Rupert Myer, chair of the Australia
    Council, as reported in the media including Chris Kenny, 'Sydney Biennale
    "Shame" Risks Funding, Says George Brandis', *The Australian*, 13 March 2014,
    and Bridie Jabour, 'George Brandis Threatens Sydney Biennale over Transfield
    "Blackballing"', *The Guardian*, 12 March 2014.

smiling alongside Council Chair, Rupert Myer. Later, Tony Grybowski, the Australia Council's CEO, and Frank Pannuci, its Executive Director, went on a tour of the state capitals to explain their agenda. They came to Adelaide on a brisk August night and handed out a nine-page document. Compared to the 151-page *Creative Australia*, it seemed a little lite-on.

Cultural policy is a funny thing. Governments of different political hues can end up continuing each other's efforts, even refining them. The Liberal Party under John Howard excoriated Paul Keating's *Creative Nation* (1994) while in opposition.[9] Once elected to office, they largely adopted its outlook. Brandis's approach in 2014 seemed initially to be a repeat of this. The Strategic Plan didn't have to be hundreds of pages long because at its elbow was the ghost of *Creative Australia*. This meant business-as-usual for artists and cultural organisations around the country: that is, government support for culture as central to a multicultural nation, Indigenous peoples, and schools and communities. If there was anything new it was the commitment to a six-year reporting cycle, which would spare a few lucky practitioners the agony of three-year grant applications.

In May 2015, the Liberal government handed down its second federal Budget. Nothing in the run-up suggested big changes for culture were afoot. But when it was delivered there was a nasty surprise. In the arts allocation, $104.7 million was diverted from the Australia Council over four years to fund a new National Programme for Excellence in the Arts (NPEA) – a 16 per cent budget cut for the agency. Since the Major Performing Arts (MPA) Framework locked in grants for 28 major cultural organisations, the money had to be taken from smaller arts organisations and project grants. The Australia Council also faced an efficiency dividend

---

9   Commonwealth of Australia, *Creative Nation* (Commonwealth Cultural Policy, October 1994).

(yet another one) of $7.2 million. Other institutions were affected: Screen Australia's funding was cut by $3.7 million, the National Gallery of Australia's by $1.5 million, the National Museum's by $600,000 and the National Portrait Gallery's by $1.7 million. All these decreases, however, were less disturbing than the NPEA itself, which appeared to do the same job as the Australia Council, only under the direct control of the minister. This undermined the nation's bipartisan history of arms-length funding, one dating back to Gough Whitlam and beyond. A war of opposing opinions bubbled up.[10]

It was a strangely hobbled debate, at first. Many cultural organisations were recipients of federal support, and so were muted in their immediate response, or, like the Australia Council, completely silent, fearing what would happen to their grants if they spoke out. For his part, Brandis hardly bothered to defend his actions. He couldn't see the fuss since, he argued; the overall funding for arts and culture would remain (roughly) the same, just delivered by a 'complementary model'.[11] The importance of the arm's-length relationship was not apparent. Perhaps it was not clear what was at stake. A few weeks after the Budget, Martin McKenzie-Murray, correspondent for the usually progressive *Saturday Paper*, commented:

> Our public debates are fractured, brimming with rancour
> and bad faith. The government's arrogance and the Left's
> vituperation have made dialectic impossible. Brandis's
> decision will be judged as cynical whimsy, or the opening
> of yet another front in the culture wars. The lack of

---

10   For a brief overview of Senator Brandis's actions, see J. Meyrick, 'The House Loses', *The Monthly*, October 2015, 11–13. For observations on the Senate Inquiry, see Meyrick and Barnett, 'Senate Inquiry into Arts Funding: Testimony and Truth in South Australia', *The Conversation*, 22 September 2015.

11   Rosemary Neill, 'Culture Shock', *The Australian*, 1 August 2015.

consultation – and the presumed contempt this reveals – will only harden enmities ... But to paraphrase French author André Gide, they should not understand him too quickly. Brandis ... has long defended government funding of the arts. This week [he] reiterated the point: 'It's an ideological view that says that the state has no business in supporting art and that's a view with which I fundamentally disagree. I think state support for art is very important, it has been enormously beneficial in building a thriving cultural sector in Australia, particularly since the Gorton government established the Australia Council in 1968'.[12]

The NPEA was duly launched, with no clear delineation of its structure and operation. The Council scrapped its plans for a six-year funding cycle and binned some other important initiatives. Together these changes provoked a grassroots campaign, Free the Arts, led by smaller arts companies and independent artists. Brandis was pilloried and satirised in pictures, cartoons and collages. Resistance to the changes grew. Some important public figures, like the philanthropist Neil Balnaves, condemned the minister's actions. George Williams, professor of constitutional law at the University of New South Wales, warned that the NPEA was vulnerable to legal challenge, saying that 'for a long time the Commonwealth assumed it could spend money on whatever it wanted ... [the High Court has] shown that to be a false view'.[13] The minister was also wrong-footed in a number of press interviews, and shown to be ignorant of the implications of his actions.[14] A Senate Inquiry into the cuts was

12 M. McKenzie-Murray, 'Inside George Brandis's Australia Council Arts Heist', *The Saturday Paper*, 23 May 2015.
13 Jane Lee, 'George Brandis's Arts Funding Program Open to Legal Challenge', *Sydney Morning Herald*, 27 July 2015.
14 See in particular Ben Eltham, 'Brandis "Completely Flummoxed" by His Own OzCo Changes', *Crikey*, 22 July 2015.

called for. It began in June 2015, and received thousands of written submissions totalling an astonishing 1.8 million words (now *that's a number*). Between August and November the Inquiry travelled around Australia, hearing testimony in 10 different hearings in nine metropolitan centres. In December, it delivered its final report, but by then Brandis was no longer Arts Minister. Malcolm Turnbull had become Prime Minister in September and reorganised his cabinet. The easy-going Mitch Fifield took over the arts portfolio, and the NPEA was renamed Catalyst. During 2016, the new body was reduced in size and scope, and some funds transferred back to the Australia Council (though it is hard to tell exactly how much of its allocation was restored). In April 2017, Catalyst was terminated and confined to history. Journalist Ben Eltham, one of Brandis's most vocal critics throughout the crisis, wrote a long essay, *When the Goal Posts Move*, which remains the best account of the entire episode. Of successive federal governments' involvement in culture he shrewdly notes:

> Within its reasonably traditional Weberian state bureaucracy, various policy spheres get treated separately and divisibly. Cultural policy is a good example. The Australia Council, nominally independent, receives its funding and imprimatur from the Arts Ministry … The Arts Ministry is a little fiefdom of its own, with its own deputy-secretary and bureaucrats (though not many of them). It currently resides within the Communications Department, but in recent years it has been shuffled about between many different parent organisations, including the Prime Minister's Department, the Regional Development portfolio and the Attorney-General's Department, as befits its mendicant status. Other silos are located further afield. The ABC … pursues its own turbulent existence as a quasi-independent body … Screen funding is disbursed through Screen

Australia, but screen tax incentives devolve ultimately from
Treasury. Copyright and intellectual property rights belong
to the Attorney-General. Australia does not have a single
'cultural czar'; even if we did, the Arts Minister would not
be she.[15]

Yet a cultural czar is exactly what Brandis sought to be. The Medici
comparison was often drawn with him, and he took obvious
pleasure in his visits to high-visibility cultural events, including the
Australian Ballet and the Venice Biennale. In other words, he acted
like a *patron* of the arts, not just a funder of them, and the untoward
appearance of the NPEA, along with Brandis's complaints that
he had 'nothing to do as a result of the arrangements left ... by
the Labor Party'[16], make complete sense when seen from this
experiential perspective.

By the same token, the Free the Arts campaign and the Senate
Inquiry allowed cultural practitioners to talk in a new way about
what they did. On 9 September, the Inquiry came to South Australia
and we were able to squeeze into the last seats in a crowded room
off a hotel lobby. For a long day, the Committee, chaired by the
independent senator and former rugby league great Glenn Lazarus,
with representation from Labor, Liberal and Greens senators,
heard from a range of individuals who spoke with an eloquence and
honesty that none of us at Laboratory Adelaide, for all our industry
experience, had heard before. (Rather than cherry-pick an example
of this outpouring, we have appended a selection at the end of this
book). The testimony was impressive – personal, but also detailed,
accurate and informed. Feeling and thought were united in articulate
statements that truthfully and movingly communicated what these

---

15   Ben Eltham, *When the Goalposts Move. Platform Paper 48* (Sydney: Currency
     Press, 2016, 25).
16   Rosemary Neill, 'Culture Shock', *The Australian*, 1 August 2015.

practitioners did and why it was important – why Australian culture was *of value* to Australia.

Now that Brandis has gone and business as usual has returned, it is worth reflecting on what his two years in the top job showed. The trouble with George was not that he was ignorant about culture, but that he knew too much and wanted something different from what was on offer. Had Brandis set up the NPEA with *new* money he might well have improved support for the arts in Australia. In the context of a cost-saving federal Budget, it would have been politically difficult. But it would have been a tiny impost compared to defence, health or social security and could have added range and flexibility to a system often resented for bureaucratic overkill. Instead he delivered a detested fiasco. For if the system for assessing and supporting Australian culture can be up-ended on little more than ministerial inclination, then it is a castle built on sand.

The Rest of this Book

The Senate Inquiry had a galvanising effect on Laboratory Adelaide. We were now convinced that the perfect number to prove the value of culture to those chronically sceptical of it was not only an impossible goal but a meaningless one. The South Australian cultural organisations we worked with directly – the State Library, the State Theatre and the Adelaide Festival – and the others we talked to, large, medium, and small, were generating metrics-saturated reports at a rate of knots. Where were these reports going? Who was reading them? Who was competent to read them? And what did 'good numbers' get you in the end? For Australia today, the nub of the problem is this: that the experience of culture is distant from its means of support. This pervasive but unacknowledged social fact is the broader context for our book, and we admit that its implications are ones we are still coming to terms with.

The chapters that follow contain more questions than answers. In the end, value isn't really 'a problem' anyway, but an aspect of being human. Despite the fact that governments treat it as interchangeable with 'benefit', it is something deeper and more resonant. Value is constitutive. It not only *is* something, it *does* something, leaving us changed as well as rewarded. Paradoxically, this is most obvious in culture, where stories of personal transformation abound. The intractability of measuring culture is offset by the fact that it sometimes embodies the very essence of the idea of value, bestowing on us a permanent enrichment of spirit. As Plato argued two and a half millennia ago, 'the soul takes nothing with her to the next world but her education and her culture'.[17]

The aim of our book is therefore simple to state, if difficult to achieve. It is to *change the conversation around the evaluation of culture in all domains*, but especially the government one, so that it reflects more context, is more honest, and makes more sense. If the impetus behind the writing is to complicate, the desired result is to facilitate better thinking and better art. But nothing is achieved by talking in an inappropriate mode of scientistic address. This is the tone of too much of the academic value literature. While the book is not personal essay, it eschews both high theory and heavy empiricism to communicate its central ideas more clearly. It seeks to engage rather than have the final word. A central assumption is that all parties involved in the creation and support of culture are of equal standing. Artists are as important as audiences, governments as important as cultural organisations. In this ecology of mutual need, no view of culture should dominate in evaluation strategies and, given the diverse forms of culture today, no view can dominate. Negotiation lies at the heart of assessment, in a process we call the 'conferral of

---

17   *The Republic*, translated by Henry Lee, 2nd edition, revised (Harmondsworth: Penguin, 1987), 63.

value', to acknowledge that however objective a metrical indicator might seem, it is only when it is socially endorsed that value can be said to exist.[18] The problem of culture's value cannot be solved in the classroom, the boardroom or the party room. It involves extended webs of social understanding and expectation. Choosing between incommensurable objectives is the bureaucrat's unenviable lot. The job of researchers is to ensure that the information available does not misrepresent the policy choices under consideration. There is a difference between helping society make easier decisions about culture, and helping it make better ones. Laboratory Adelaide's commitment is to the latter.

The structure of the book is relatively simple. The first chapter addresses definitions of key terms. Thereafter follow three brief case studies from different cultural domains ('The Problems'). Here, we discuss what we call 'parables of value', looking at cultural experience *in situ*, and identifying the difficulties and challenges these examples throw up for anyone serious about evaluating them. The second part of the book ('Where to from Here?') looks at how we might address such difficulties and challenges by developing a new sensitivity to language and narrative. We then draw attention to recent trends in evaluation and reporting occurring in the corporate sector. The conclusion makes some broad remarks about the social structures that have given rise to the problem of value in its contemporary, desiccated form. But it would be depressing, and perhaps misleading, to end the book on this note, so we finish with the words of some of the hundreds of people who made submissions to the 2015 Senate Inquiry into the Brandis arts cuts.

A deep conviction the authors share is that there can be no over-determining, abstract view of culture. It has to take place in some

---

18   J. Meyrick, T. Barnett and R. Phiddian, 'The Conferral of Cultural Value', *Media International Australia*. Under review.

place, at some time, and within distinctive social arrangements. Broad conclusions about culture can be made, but always need translation to and from particular contexts. For us, Adelaide is a fine city to take as a reference point. Bigger than small but smaller than big, it has one of everything by way of major cultural organisations, and a longstanding commitment to the arts. It has the Dunstan legacy: the remarkable Premier of South Australia, Don Dunstan – he of the pink shorts and safari suits – who in the 1970s brought the city and its culture to a point of identity. South Australia is 'the Festival State', in its heart as well as on its car licence plates, and while it currently faces tough economic times, culturally it boxes above its weight. For this reason, our book is relentlessly 'glocal', taking its examples from the Adelaide cultural scene while mining these for insights that are more widely applicable. The exception (in focus and to some extent in tone) is the chapter 'The Reporting of Value' at the end, which describes new international accounting frameworks as a practical way forward.

Laboratory Adelaide is a project with its roots firmly in the humanities. As researchers we come from the creative arts, literary criticism and digital studies. Our work connects with social scientific approaches to value, but the expertise we bring derives from the cultural disciplines. We are, consequently, particularly sensitive to issues of language. It is possible to measure things that cannot be defined precisely. The validity of numerical data when everyone's understanding of key terms is different, however, is open to doubt. This is not a problem more information will fix. 'Big data' often makes the task of aligning words and numbers more difficult, bringing blindness as well as insight. The message of our little book is therefore 'stop measuring and judge carefully'. If we are serious as a society about assessing culture's value, we need to accept the difficulty of the task and the limited nature of the proofs. Culture is a varied and constantly changing phenomenon; value is a profound conception of human gain. As researchers we need a degree of intellectual humility – something usually missing from the measurement debate – a catholicity of taste, and an ambition to be as flexible in recognising forms of value, as cultural practitioners are in creating them.

Box 1 'The Funding Game': A (Very) Brief History Lesson

In the last half-century, arts and culture in Australia have been dominated by government policy and government agencies. Yet the public funding of culture does not go back much further than 1950. It is worth keeping this history in mind. Government is big in the Australian cultural sector, but not eternally so. Its influence could wane again. That may, in fact, be what happens in the twenty-first century.

In the sixty years after Federation there were modest cultural initiatives like the Commonwealth Literary Fund (established 1908), the ABC orchestras (established 1932–36), the Elizabethan Theatre Trust (established 1954), as well as state-funded libraries, art galleries, museums and, with the long and finally triumphant saga of the Sydney Opera House, concert halls. However, it was not until the founding of the Australian Council for the Arts in 1968, and a major expansion of funding in 1973, that Australia had an arts policy with the resources to make things happen.

There are good reasons why it was needed. Following waves of postwar migration, Australia could no longer see itself as a cultural extension of Britain, but the initiative to recognise this change could not come from the commercial sector, which was fundamentally risk-averse (and still is). Moreover, Australians have traditionally looked to government for leadership, and there was no strong philanthropic support base, despite relatively high levels of prosperity (again, still the case). A distinctive national culture was not going to occur spontaneously. A range of government programs at federal and state levels were developed to address this.

Despite being publicly funded, at first artists were largely left to evaluate their work themselves in a combination of peer review and an arm's length relationship from politicians. But Australia's turn towards neo-liberal beliefs in the 1980s exerted an influence on all it touched. Money spent on arts and culture had to be justified in budgets that might otherwise spend it on healthcare, education, or manufacturing. Art for art's sake is not a plausible policy criterion in an environment dominated by audit rigour and value-for-money. The 'governmentalisation' of the arts, as policy critic Lisanne Gibson has called it, is a logical consequence of artists having economic rationalist governments as a patron. Its budget processes require general explanations, abstract justifications, statistical proofs. These are often hard for cultural practitioners to provide, because the meaning of their work resides in the personal response it evokes. Government evaluation strategies seek to be detached and objective. Neither parameter is relevant when you want to write the great Australian novel.

The introduction of more instrumental assessment methods for the arts started in 1976, when the Industries Assistance Commission handed down its report *Assistance to the Performing Arts*, acidly suggesting the sector should be treated 'like any other service industry'. Prime Minister Malcolm Fraser did not follow its econometric recommendations. But arts and culture have been squaring off against this policy dynamic ever since. In the subsequent 40-plus years, Australian governments have initiated a number of inquiries and reports into the sector (see our Brief Chronology below). In 1981, the first major economic analysis of Australian culture appeared, Kenneth Tollhurst's 'Australians' Attitudes to the Arts'. Thereafter, there was a rush to produce economic impact studies, though whether these found genuine traction, either with the Treasury officials who questioned their assumptions, or with the artists who saw them as tangential to their artistic goals, is moot.

In 1994, the Keating government released *Creative Nation,* marking a shift from an 'arts policy' to a 'cultural policy', with the widening of scope this implies. In tone and intent it is a very different document from *Assistance to the Performing Arts.* Yet it retains a preoccupation with the contribution of culture to the economy as 'a valuable export in itself and an essential accompaniment to the export of our commodities'. It declares that 'the level of our creativity substantially determines our ability to adapt to new economic imperatives'. This focus continues in our last national cultural policy, *Creative Australia,* in 2013.

Not only art and culture's economic contribution, but its social, educational and wellbeing 'spill overs' are now the objects of an industry of evidenced-based research by governments, academics and the sector itself. None of this data is without use, but it is problematic. We end up evaluating things that have little to do with qualities intrinsic to culture, its production, and its experience. Nor does the strategy seem to be working, as support for arts and culture is almost the only area of public expenditure going backwards, according to *The Australian* newspaper's economics correspondent David Uren (26 May 2016). Australian society may have beaten a retreat from Whitlam's national-culture-building vision, but it is worth considering the 'funding game' critically, and whether there are alternatives. As one artist wrote to us recently, in a private communication:

> The money is swiftly running out. Always living down to the line. It's an old familiar feeling. However, as I finish writing up my final grant acquittal, I realise that once it is approved I am free from the cycle of arts funding. Each time I am tempted to apply for an upcoming round, I step away and do something else. It is not a sustainable future, not for me, not for anyone. [...] What is missing is the idea of 'investment' and 'return'. The only thing

that keeps happening is artists 'return' for more grants!
And the pool of applications is getting larger by the
round. What I've learnt is that there is no actual logic to
arts funding. There are no resulting outcomes apart from
keeping individuals, groups and organisations hanging
on for subsequent rounds, hoping their number will come
up. I realise that funding is a privilege and not a right. But
to me, after almost 15 years, there is no follow-through,
with arts funding bodies probably knowing full well the
majority of artists can never achieve independent financial
status. The logic is skewed because one cannot just apply
to be 'supported'. The majority of funds have to go to
various strands of production and the applying artist ends
up getting the left-overs (aside from fellowships, which as
we know are singular occurrences). I feel there could be
a much better way of spending government money on
artists. I believe the solution is something like a 10-year
period of base income funding [for those] who have shown
consistency in their practice rather than this grab-bag of
amounts that just go around in circles.

Brief Chronology of Formal Australian Cultural Policy since Federation in 1901

1908   Commonwealth Literary Fund, Australia's first government cultural subsidy fund established.

1947   Guthrie Report on the state of Australian theatre.

1954   Australian Elizabethan Theatre Trust, predecessor of the Australia Council for the Arts, established.

1963   Vincent Report on the state of Australian film.

1968   The Australian Council for the Arts established by Holt–Gorton Coalition government.

WHAT MATTERS?

1972   Gough Whitlam becomes both Prime Minister and federal Arts Minister in the first Labor government for 23 years.

1973   Whitlam announces plans for a new national cultural agency, the Australia Council. Federal arts budget increases from $7 million to $14 million. H.C. 'Nugget' Coombs, former Governor of the Reserve Bank, becomes first Chair of the Council.

1974   Legislation introduced into federal parliament to give the Australia Council statutory independence.

1975   Australia Council Act passed. Whitlam's Labor government ousted from office in November ('The Dismissal').

1976   The Industries Assistance Commission hands down its report Assistance to the Performing Arts.

1986   The House of Representatives Standing Committee on Expenditure hands down Patronage, Power and the Muse (the McLeay Report).

1989   Following the recommendation of the McLeay Report, the Australia Council establishes a Major Organisations Board. The first triennial grants are introduced.

1994   Creative Nation launched by Prime Minister Paul Keating's Labor government.

2000–01   Securing the Future (the Nugent Report) handed down by Prime Minister John Howard's Coalition government.

2013   Creative Australia launched by Prime Minister Julia Gillard's Labor government.

Part I

THE PROBLEMS

CHAPTER ONE

Some Definitions

'Remarks aren't literature.'
Gertrude Stein

They aren't systematic analysis either, and this short book does not present a comprehensive academic treatise on assaying the problem of culture's value. Nor is it a how-to guide, a Culture for Dummies, giving tactical advice on grant submission or the use of quantitative data in policy-making. Rather, it offers what Howard Becker in his seminal work *Art Worlds* calls 'a complication',[1] a series of commentaries on the question of value as it appears in a technologically advanced, socially diverse culture like Australia. The impetus to write it comes from the belief that the act of valuing culture, as opposed to the act of creating it in the first place, is one that modern democracies do very badly. The tables, targets, and tracking we typically employ do not help, and probably hinder, a true understanding of what culture means to us and the decisions we need to make about it. It sounds provocative, but is a good place to start, to ask whether, objectively speaking, the evaluative strategies favoured by governments today are so counterproductive that it would be better if they did nothing at all to assess how their money is spent. The results are not just a waste of time. They actively

---

1   Howard Becker, *Art Worlds* (Berkeley: University of California Press, 1982), viii.

mislead because they suggest they are definitively measuring something when often they reveal only the ingrained belief that anything can be definitively measured. Metric power is ascendant in large part because people assent to its seldom-tested assumptions. Though perhaps that assent may be finally weakening.

There is a way ahead, but it is not by spraying out numbers in the belief they speak for themselves. They do not. They are made to speak by the words around them and the rhetorical purpose for which they are arranged. They can be deployed honestly and forensically, or distortingly and duplicitously, and to many other ends. Hence, the relationship between words and numbers is a crucial axis of attention in evaluating cultural activities and discriminating between them with regards to their public support. This sets useful limits on the over-claiming of quantitative data by demanding relevant context around its application. *What does a number mean?* is the most important question anyone can ask in an era which is able, like ours, to snow citizens with unlimited formulas and figures.[2] Restoring a balance between how we describe culture verbally and how we count it numerically is an intrinsically important goal. *Right You Are (If You Think So)* is the title of a 1917 play by Italian dramatist Luigi Pirandello in which two people accuse each other of being mad and a group of citizens have to discover which one is telling the truth. Evidence is refuted by evidence, explanation by explanation, in a plot that has no final resolution. Truth is elusive, but the quest for it triggers growth. Some things don't have easy answers, 'just' a capacity to generate important questions. So it is with culture. Asking 'What value does culture have?' is an act that can add value in itself. It will not lead, via big data, to an algorithm that will make our judgments for us. Instead, the process of evaluation can assist

---

2   See Cathy O'Neil, *Weapons of Math Destruction: How Big Data Increases Inequality and Threatens Democracy* (New York: Crown, 2016).

engaging with culture in a more meaningful way. All the more reason not to leave matters where they stand, with data replacing experience, and the widespread but erroneous belief that culture can be properly measured without first being properly understood.

The Culture of Culture

Certain words denote certain things. Other words denote things other than themselves. 'Culture' is a word that carries meanings of all kinds. In *Metaphors We Live By*, George Lakoff and Mark Johnson show how some words we use on a daily basis structure our understanding of quite different phenomena. They give examples. Argument is war. Time is money. Love is a journey. 'The essence of metaphor', they say, 'is understanding and experiencing one thing in terms of another'.[3] Their book is now 35 years old, which probably explains why the meteoric rise of culture as a metaphor for almost every area of contemporary social life is not included. Today, culture is everywhere, not because everything is culture, but because the word itself is used in a seemingly limitless range of situations to cover an unruly tribe of ideas and instances. We have the culture of sport, the culture of education, and the culture of business. The culture of lending in the banking industry is under the microscope, as is the culture of misogyny and sexual harassment in the corporate sector as a whole. There is a culture of bullying in schools, a culture of binge drinking outside them, and a culture of fear in our CBDs as a result. Interaction between genders is a matter of culture, as are relations between religions and between academic disciplines.

---

3   George Lakoff and Mark Johnson, *Metaphors We Live By* (Chicago: University of Chicago Press, 1980), 5.

We have cultures of victimhood, cultures of blame, cultures of forgetting, cultures of safety, and cultures of risk. Being innovative is a matter of culture ('a culture of innovation'), as is being excellent ('a culture of quality'). There are cultures of peace, cultures of violence, cultures of silence, and Robert Hughes's well-known cultures of complaint.[4] Stick the word 'culture' into Google search, and it will return 1,680,000,000 results in 0.43 seconds. 'Truth' returns just 627,000,000, and even 'God' only 1,280,000,000. A vast number of books have 'culture' in their title. The National Library of Australia lists 1,827 in its main catalogue, plus a further 80 journals. In 2014, 'culture' was the most looked-up term in the Merriam-Webster dictionary. Confusion about culture, the New York journalist Joshua Rothman observed, 'is just part of the culture … The problem is that the word … is more than the sum of its definitions'.[5]

Culture's complex metaphorical application means the word is often at odds with the factual face peering into the research mirror. 'The shoe of shoe' is a sort of philosophical joke, a rumination on the tension between 'essence' and 'existence', perhaps. 'The culture of culture' is a statement that at first glance makes sense. It seems to say something, at least potentially. It offers not a subject of contemplation but an object for investigation. What kind of culture does culture have? Are there things that make some kinds of culture cultur*al* as opposed to other kinds that self-evidently don't? Anthropologists, sociologists, psychologists and critical thinkers enter here, with their theories, models, surveys, comparative analyses and statistics.

---

4   Robert Hughes, *Culture of Complaint: The Fraying of America* (New York: Oxford University Press, 1993).

5   Joshua Rothman, 'The Meaning of "Culture"', *The New Yorker*, 26 December 2014.

Like the Magic Pudding, culture is endlessly divisible along disciplinary lines, and yet, hey presto, there is always more of it to go round. A master-theory of culture would already exist if it were soluble by incremental research, given the person-years devoted to it but, like 'the answer to Shakespeare', it is not that sort of question. This remains true even if you narrow your investigation to the older senses of culture anchored to the arts and humanities. Is it an object? A process? A relation? Is culture something that exists in the world or in our heads? If a bit of both, what are the boundaries and the arrows of causation? Is culture a singular or a collective experience? Can I decide when something is culture or is general consensus required?

If I read a book that everyone hates but I like, am I culturally in the wrong? Are cultural opinions a matter of demonstrable proof, like scientific opinions? Or plausible belief, like legal ones? Or are they simply expressions of consumer preference, such as a taste for mustard over tomato sauce, or blue walls over green? If the last, then the significance of the word hardly seems to justify the ink spilled over it. Yet clearly culture plays an important role in our lives. How to understand that role and improve it? One response is 'Should we even try?' If culture is a term of flat description, then there can be, logically, no improvement in it, only what the Reserve Bank calls 'quantitative easing' – the provision of more or less of certain cultural goods and services. But here, like a draught of cold air from the floorboards, comes a nagging reminder this is *not* all that culture stands for, that it is, in the words of the half-forgotten American literary critic Lionel Trilling,

> an idea of great attractiveness and undoubted usefulness.
> We may say it begins in the assumption that all human
> expressions or artifacts are indicative of some considerable
> tendencies in the life of social groups ... and that which

is indicative is also causative – all cultural facts have their consequences. To think in cultural terms is to consider human expressions not only in their own existence and avowed intention, but in, as it were, their secret life, taking cognisance of the desires and impulses which lie behind the open formulation ... The concept of culture affords to those who use it a sense of liberation ... for they deal less with abstractions and mere objects, more with the momentous actualities of human feelings as these shape and condition the human community, as they make and as they indicate the quality of man's existence. Not the least of the attractions of the cultural mode of thought are the passions which attend it – because it assumes that all things are causative or indicative of the whole of the cultural life, it proposes to us those intensities of moralised feeling which seem appropriate to our sense that all that is good in life is at stake in every cultural action ... We can ... no more escape from the cultural mode of thought than we can escape from culture itself.[6]

There is Culture as Thing, but also Culture as Category, what Trilling calls 'the cultural mode of thought', and for him at least there is no escaping its normative implications.[7] Culture has about it a quality of 'ought': what we *ought* to be reading, watching, listening to, experiencing, at least part of the time. For some people this is already fusty elitism, an indefensible elevation of certain activities above others, when choice should be individual and free. Why should books be preferred to baton-twirling, opera to soap opera, interior design to tattoo design? But this is not what Trilling is saying. The

---

6   Lionel Trilling, *Beyond Culture: Essays on Literature and Learning* (New York: Viking Press, 1965), 173–75.
7   See also Lionel Trilling, 'Science, Literature and Culture: A Comment on the Leavis–Snow Controversy', *Higher Education Quarterly*, 17, no. 1 (1962): 9–32.

cultural mode of thought pulls towards deep and common (if not necessarily universal) experiences. It allows us to talk and speculate about the biggest of big pictures – Life with a capital 'L'. Arguably, Tolstoy, George Eliot and Samuel Beckett do just that. Arguably so do Ella Fitzgerald, Margaret Atwood and Snoop Dogg. The point is not who or what is at the top of an imagined cultural league table – the respectable term is 'canon' – but the fact that we can't help making such discriminations ourselves. If we didn't, all CDs, books, and films would sell equally, or reflect changes in exogenous factors only. But they don't, because we don't buy them on the basis of a price x quantity algorithm. We buy them on the basis of liking some things more than others, and knowing full well this reflects surges in the collective consciousness. We also judge some things to be better than others, and find various ways to talk to others about that, in terms that used to be called cultural criticism.

Many people have written on the meaning of the word culture, of which perhaps Matthew Arnold is the oldest, and Raymond Williams the best known. Arnold, poet, polemicist and school inspector, published his famous book *Culture and Anarchy* in 1869. In it, he called culture 'a pursuit of our total perfection by means of getting to know, on all the matters which most concern us, the best that has been said and thought in the world and, through this knowledge, turning a stream of fresh and free thought upon our stock notions and habits'.[8] Here, culture is implicitly associated with certain things, ones we tend to call, and which they call themselves, 'the arts'. It is a restricted definition and leaves out many of the activities that a broader interpretation would see as having a legitimate cultural dimension to them. It is also limited in the consideration it shows matters of class, race and gender. With

---

8   Matthew Arnold, *Culture and Anarchy*, ed. Jane Garnett (Oxford: Oxford University Press, 2006), 5.

this in mind, Williams published an influential essay, 'Culture is Ordinary', in 1958, in which he observed that

> When I now read a book such as Clive Bell's *Civilisation,* I experience not so much disagreement as stupor. What kind of life can it be, I wonder, to produce this extraordinary fussiness, this extraordinary decision to call certain things culture and then separate them, as with a park wall, from ordinary people and ordinary work? At home we met and made music, listened to it, recited and listened to poems, valued fine language. I heard better music and better poems since; there is the world to draw on. But I know, from the most ordinary experience, that the interest is there, the capacity is there ... Culture is ordinary: through every change let us hold fast to that.[9]

This is a different view. Though Williams had time for Arnold, he disagreed with the premise that culture should be identified with the high arts, and that these could be hierarchically ranked like an army regiment.[10] Williams's understanding of theatre and film was detailed and extensive. 'Culture is Ordinary' is not a lazy, 'anything goes' response to Arnoldian claims for art-as-culture. Nor is it flatly materialist like economic rationalist approaches. There is still an 'ought' in Williams, but it is of a different kind from Arnold's: a life-as-culture 'ought' that is no less imperative and which is strongly opposed to the deadening mechanisation and social stratification of twentieth century capitalism. From Arnold, we get formalist schools of aesthetic inquiry. He had a profound effect on FR Leavis, the literary critic, who in turn influenced generations of English

9   Raymond Williams, 'Culture is Ordinary', in *Resources of Hope: Culture, Democracy, Socialism* (London: Verso Books, 1989), 94.
10   See also Raymond Williams, *Culture and Society, 1780–1950* (Harmondsworth: Penguin, 1993).

teachers, and Williams himself, in the techniques of close textual analysis. Williams, after he broke with Leavis, allied himself with Richard Hoggart and Stuart Hall from the Birmingham Centre of Contemporary Cultural Studies, whose approach to culture was informed by sociology and social theory. From these two disciplinary traditions – there are others, but they have been the most influential in Australian intellectual life[11] – arise what might be called the narrow and the broad understandings of Trilling's cultural mode of thought.

Over the last 50 years, these two schools have spent considerable time and energy bagging each other. The rise of cultural studies, in Australia and elsewhere, would have been a non-event without this antagonism, and there are echoes of it in the recently established Ramsay Centre for Western Civilisation, with a generous endowment to support the Arnold end of the debate. We do not re-engage the debate here. There are strengths on both sides, and important areas of shared concern. Instead, we accept the fact that culture is simultaneously everywhere and somewhere. It is found in particular objects and activities, and also in everything human beings encounter on a daily basis. Culture is a part of what philosophers call 'the commons'. Indeed, it is their emotional core and psychological ground. The pervasiveness of culture means that, like gravity, it is both 'weak' (hard to define and measure) and all-powerful (the thing that holds other things together).

This is a state of affairs we choose. With Trilling, we choose to use the word 'culture' to refer to 'actualities of human feelings as these shape and condition the human community', and a lot more besides. We could use different words for different things, but we don't because we are interested in what they share – the having

---

11 See Peter Goodall, *High Culture, Popular Culture: The Long Debate* (Sydney: Allen & Unwin, 1995).

of a thing called culture. And if this creates problems because culture's meaning is so elastic as to suggest few concrete traits and no precise range, that's a choice too. We choose to be vaguely right rather than precisely wrong, sensing that calling something culture is not like awarding a sports day rosette, but is the first step in a longer process of investigation and assessment. The cultural mode of thought is a broad affiliation. What we lose in semantic purchase we gain in cognitive flexibility. Things we would struggle to describe can attract this handy term. The Australian Securities and Investment Commission (ASIC) identified what it called 'breaches of the financial services culture' in the Australian banking sector.[12] Opposing ASIC's extension of the criminal code to the Corporations Act, John Colvin argued that culture is 'a nebulous concept and has evaded a comprehensive definition'.[13] Well, yes. But ASIC's deployment of the word was less concerned with proposing definitions than highlighting problems. The meaning is the use, in Wittgenstein's famous phrase, and our use of 'culture' today is of the broadest and most fundamental kind.

The Value of Value

The equation of the value of a thing with its market price is the subject of strong and repeated censure in the Hebrew and Christian Scriptures. In the Book of Job, we find the following:

> Where shall wisdom be found? …
> Man knoweth not the price thereof …
> It cannot be gotten for gold, neither shall
> silver be weighed [for] the price thereof. It cannot

---

12 'O'Dwyer Backs ASIC Action on Bank Culture', *Sydney Morning Herald*, 21 March 2016.
13 'Culture Is Too Hard to Regulate', *Australian Financial Review*, 7 March 2016.

be valued with the gold of Ophir, with the precious onyx, or
the sapphire. The gold and the crystal cannot equal
it: and the exchange of it [shall not be for] jewels or fine
gold. No mention shall be made of coral, or of
pearls: for the price of wisdom [is] above rubies.
The topaz of Ethiopia shall not equal it, neither shall it be
valued with pure gold. Whence then cometh
wisdom? and where [is] the place of understanding?
… Behold, the
fear of the Lord, that [is] wisdom; and to depart from evil
[is] understanding. (Job 28, 12–20 and 28)[14]

While 'culture' has been rapidly conquering new semantic territories
in recent decades, the word 'value' has declined in its associations
and significance. Historically, what was a rich, multidimensional
term evoking a range of thoughts, feelings and perspectives has
been stripped of its layers of meaning and increasingly used to
signify one thing only: financial value. This has been a matter of
shrinkage, of ever-narrower and less qualitative constructions
of value. The point is made by David Throsby, one of the world's
leading cultural economists:

[In] the twentieth century … in economics, theory acquired
a new axiomatic rigor. Price expressed in monetary terms
was identified with the impartial result of all the subjective
and objective variables that impinge on any transaction.
A new hierarchy was established wherein price and value
became synonymous; in this logical universe, cultural
and artistic value were seen as a subjective category,
beyond the scope of scientific inquiry. In Debreu's (1959)

---

14   The Bible: the-holy-bible-king-james-version.soft32.com/free-download.

canonical version, *value* [was] defined as 'market price times commodity volume'.[15]

Value was once something to be discriminated; that is, discerned according to critical judgment. Today, we are happier when it can be counted. Where numbers really are meaningful, this constitutes progress. But that is a heavy proviso, and culture is a zone where metrical proxies are frequently tendentious, used to mask opinions rather than inform them. That masking takes the form of a spurious hard-headedness that reduces value to limited instrumental outcomes, classically a dollar figure. The cartoon by Jon Kudelka on the front cover of this book captures the problem perfectly. Liberal Senator James Paterson reacted to a valuation of Jackson Pollock's *Blue Poles* at $350 million by suggesting the government sell it to retire debt. Any ascribed dollar amount is a minor part of the value to the nation of this controversial and collection-defining work of art. When assessing it, you cannot assume it is equivalent to 210,853.535 troy ounces of gold.[16] Gold exists in an economic market; a work of abstract expressionism exists in a history of meaning. It is arguable that the Ned Kelly series by Sidney Nolan or the 'Aboriginal Memorial' that haunts the foyer of the National Gallery of Australia are even more valuable. But it is arguable because it is part of a story through which we understand ourselves, not because we can charge 'what the market will bear'.

An important discussion of the evolution of the idea of value (the value of value) can be found in Jane Gleeson-White's 2014 work *Six Capitals*. This is the sequel to her history of financial accounting

---

15 Michael Hutter and David Throsby, eds, *Beyond Price: Value in Culture, Economics, and the Arts* (Melbourne: Cambridge University Press, 2008, 2 (original italics).

16 The spot-price for $350,000,000 of gold on 6 November 2017.

practices, *Double Entry*,[17] which appeared a few years previously. Together, the two books provide a readily accessible exploration of the relationship between value and monetised metrics. Gleeson-White discusses the challenges facing those who strive to measure the value of intangible things, such as intellectual ideas, or non-renewable ones, like natural resources. For accountants, these present as problems of asset valuation, which are usually transposed into financial terms. The double entry accounting system expresses liabilities in the same way, so that firms (or nations) can align assets alongside liabilities and 'see' whether they are running at a profit or a loss. Since the fourteenth century, accounting practices have become a deal more sophisticated, allowing for deeper understanding of fiscal operations. But accounting's idea of value has not undergone radical reform, and remains in essence that which can be expressed financially on a balance sheet. Some things lend themselves to this calculative approach more than others, so accountants have developed different conceptions of 'capital' to reckon the manufacturing, human and social dimensions of economic life as these complicate the process of wealth accumulation. In *Six Capitals*, Gleeson-White discusses two international reporting frameworks that have recently emerged as a way of better accounting for the value of factors that elude quantitative measure.

We return to Global Reporting Initiative (GRI) and Integrated Reporting (<IR>) later in the book to examine their potential for culture. For now, what matters is that the ambition to turn all that we do and have into 'an asset' of one kind or another is extremely contentious. It puts forward not only a *process* of value, but also a *metaphor* for it. By treating each entity in a way that makes it exchangeable with another – economists talk about 'substitutability',

---

17   Jane Gleeson-White, *Double Entry: How the Merchants of Venice Shaped the Modern World – and How Their Invention Could Make or Break the Planet* (Sydney: Allen & Unwin, 2011).

accountants about 'fungibility' – it places all phenomena on a plane of theoretical equivalence. A native forest could be valued 'the same as' a local golf course, or a family friend 'the same as' a family home. We recoil at such equivalences as intellectually and morally dubious. Yet modern society makes such calculations on a daily basis. Actuaries and insurance brokers regularly put a price on objects, persons and relations we would regard as irreplaceable but which are treated as things that can be weighed and measured in standardised units, and thus compared. In 2016, the Art Gallery of South Australia announced that its collection had been valued at over a billion dollars and was the largest asset in the state[18]. It is a spurious figure, both because the collection will never be put on the market, and because it would create a glut of artworks that would never return this hypothetical book value if an attempt were made to sell them. Even flat-broke US cities like Detroit and Buffalo have rejected the idea of selling great public art collections gathered in their glory days. Under stress, citizens and politicians still believe art has more than a dollar value. They are surely right.

Weighing and measuring is necessarily an act of comparison. Things that are not other things are placed in a common category of description, compared and counted together (or contrasted and excluded from the count). Categorisation must happen *before* measurement can take place and carries with it the implied belief that a thing both *can* be measured and *should* be measured by way of accounting for its value. This belief can be wrong. The film *Schindler's List* is in part a study of corrupt calculative practices, of how the counting of something – the nominative category of being Jewish – can be harnessed to immoral and criminal ends. The equation of value with price seems more innocent, but there are dark undertows.

---

18   'Call for new site as Art Gallery of SA collection revalued at $1bn'. Adelaide Now, 26 August, 2016.

Gleeson-White suggests that George Monbiot, the journalist and environmental activist,

> regards the very idea of giving the natural world financial value as a sign of defeat, a way of framing an argument for the inherent value of nature and its preservation in the terms of ... those who seek to destroy it in the name of economic development. He [Monbiot] writes, 'Costing nature tells us that it possesses no inherent value; that it is worthy of protection only when it performs services for us; that it is replaceable. You demoralise and alienate those who love the natural world while reinforcing the values of those who don't.' Monbiot's argument ... stopped me in my tracks. It fed into my growing misgivings about how would nature benefit from its reconception as natural capital and sparked a dawning realisation of the full implications – moral, aesthetic and spiritual – of these persuasive ... moves to price nature in order to save it ... It brought home to me the full force of Keynes' 1933 remark 'once we allow ourselves to be disobedient to the test of an accountant's profit, we have begun to change our civilisation', and of the true bankruptcy of a civilisation which has so lost its bearings in the universe that its only apparent common measure of value, and of right or wrong action, is the rule of money.[19]

What Monbiot and Gleeson-White say about costing nature is transferrable to arts and culture. Trying to speak 'the language of government' confirms their instrumentalism and 'demoralises and alienates' those who love the arts (including oneself). To win funding battles, the whole terrain of meaningful evaluation is conceded.

---

19 Gleeson-White, *Six Capitals*, 88–89; see also George Monbiot, 'Can You Put a Price on the Beauty of the Natural World?', *The Guardian*, April 22, 2014.

The basic premise of cultural economics is that a distinction can be made between culture's economic value and its other forms of value and that these can be estimated in monetary terms separately. This allows some push back against the dodgy equivalences of financial accounting. Yet, as Gleeson-White suggests, despite the fact that we have developed sophisticated ideas of return in different areas of the economy, capital keeps slipping back to an identification with money, and money keeps slipping back to an identification with value. Like the environment, representing culture as a problem of value reveals dissatisfaction with the neo-liberal beliefs of Western society over the past 30 years. These beliefs are still dominant, but are beginning to show wear and tear.[20]

Just as you cannot solve the problem of culture's meaning by haggling over definitions, you cannot solve the problem of its value with more measurement techniques. The proposition that a better index of measurement by itself furnishes a better idea of value is not only false, it imparts falsity to the propositions around it, creating a bank of spurious knowledge, a phrenology of culture. Epistemological questions (questions of knowledge) come second to social ones (questions of collective belief), since there is always a social context to the measurement techniques we deploy. That social context provides a consensus that something of value exists prior to it being investigated more systematically. This is important when studying things we cannot see, like quantum particles, or which have no corporeal existence, like the national economy, or exist as abstract concepts, like justice. Arguably, culture falls into all three camps. We can say 'we aren't measuring culture well enough' or 'our idea of value is too instrumental', but the issue is more fundamental.

---

20 See, for example, William Davies, *The Limits of Neoliberalism* (London: Sage, 2014) and Paul Mason, *Postcapitalism: A Guide to Our Future* (London: Allen Lane, 2015).

The truth is there isn't enough substance on the problem when it arrives in the public domain.

There seems to be a growing awareness of this unsatisfactory state of affairs, even among major accountancy firms like Deloitte and KPMG, both of whom have approached Laboratory Adelaide to discuss these issues. The way forward lies not in synthesising a humungous metrical model for computing culture's absolute value, but in finding a better balance between concrete examples and analytical concepts. On this score, Bruno Latour has some sharp things to say about the social sciences:

> You never have a chemistry class that starts with the methodology of chemistry; you start by doing chemistry. And the problem is that since the social sciences don't know what it is to be scientific … they imagine that they have to be listing endless numbers of criteria and precautions before doing anything. They usually miss precisely what is interesting in natural sciences, which is a laboratory situation and the experimental protocol.[21]

This suggests that approaches to measuring culture's value today, which often rely just on methodological self-consciousness, are ineffective; that while they may bolster our sense of mastery over a tricky area, they do little to illuminate it. But no-one is off the hook. Governments, artists, journalists and researchers all face the same crenelated landscape, where proving culture's worth to any but an immediately sympathetic cohort is difficult. Thus, while we all know that culture has an important inherent value – consider the global outcry to the horrifying Charlie Hebdo killings in Paris,

---

21   Bruno Latour, Graham Harman and Peter Erdélyi, *The Prince and the Wolf: Latour and Harman at the LSE* (London: John Hunt Publishing, 2011), 79–80.

or the terrible destruction of the Temple of Bel in Palmyra[22] – we have no means of anchoring it in our public consciousness. Talk about inherent value ends up either so broad as to be specious, or so particular as to sound like special pleading. It is not that we don't know what we are saying when we make a case for culture's culture, it is that we can't ground it in a deep enough understanding of value's value. This is why our evaluative strategies keep collapsing into the measurement of economic and social effects. And that is unfortunate, since the problem of culture's value is a subset of the larger problem of value in society, and properly understanding it is key not only to better cultural policy but to a better life. In this book our focus is not on measurement methods but on how culture is talked about and how it talks about itself. It is in the histories and patterns of sociability around measurement processes that we may find a way to combat what Michael Pusey in his book *Economic Rationalism in Canberra* (1991) calls a 'transcontextual commensurability of reference'.[23] This accommodation may not satisfy Monbiot, but it will allow more detail to inform evaluative strategies, complicating but also improving our idea of culture's value and its assessment.

---

22 For an analysis of the Charlie Hebdo killings, see Julian Meyrick, Robert Phiddian and Richard Maltby, 'The Mocking of the Modern Mind: Culture and Cartooning in the Age of Je suis Charlie Hebdo', *Australian Book Review*, April 2015, 47–49.

23 Michael Pusey, *Economic Rationalism in Canberra: A Nation-building State Changes its Mind* (Melbourne: Cambridge University Press, 1991), 11.

Box 2 Parables of Value

Anecdotes are slippery things. A well-chosen anecdote can give a politician or an artist a peg on which to hang a commitment many times larger and more complex than the simple story that has 'sold' it. By contrast, dismissing something as 'anecdotal' can consign the arguments around it to oblivion. Is there a more stable way of anchoring the value of arts and culture than the rhetorical roulette of whether an anecdote hits its target?

We propose bridging the gap between 'objective' evidence and 'subjective' opinion by using what we call 'parables of value' – narratives that illuminate the issues at stake in a way abstract data cannot. A transformational childhood experience of reading in a public library speaks powerfully to the value of libraries. It is a story of a single person's experience, yes, statistically indistinguishable from the child who visited the library to find the photocopier broken and nothing useful for her school assignment. But it is exemplary of the library's purpose. The narrative has to be there, beside the numerical tables on footfalls and productivity measures, to explain what a library actually *does*. Evaluation must balance abstract, aggregate measures of frequency with personal experience.

There is considerable overlap between academic researchers' use of case studies and our conception of parables of value. Any competent case study will have a parabolic dimension to it, as it must tell a story exemplifying a wider set of relations or conditions. Such an approach is not an exercise in make-believe, but a discipline of framing evidence meaningfully and holistically so readers get a sense of what is at stake in human terms without being in a particular situation themselves.

For assessment processes, parables of value can also enhance (or even eliminate) the rote mission statement. A handful of parables can reflect a cultural organisation's commitments more profoundly than a list of abstract nouns. They can give a window into the artistic experiences an organisation aims to foster.

There are limits to storytelling, and the potential for mis-framing as well as for elucidation. For parables of value to be more than an invitation to bullshit, they must have principles of both form and function. These principles require good faith and must be policed by a degree of critical awareness.

To be used in assessment processes, parables of value should be:

- **Truthful**. Parables should describe events that happened and can be verified in their basics.
- **Apposite.** Parables should relate narratives that bear on the core purposes of an organisation, program or project, and that connection should be easily shown.
- **Significant.** Parables may relate peak events or typical experiences, and need not be representative of an organisation's whole profile. But they cannot refer to outlier occcurences in what they describe.
- **Concise.** Jesus set an impressive standard in the Gospels that few organisations today can equal. Parables should draw their meaning from the context around them, and not spend much time in scene-setting. They need to be graspable in a couple of minutes, and might reasonably be given strict word limits in official assessment.
- **Relevant.** Parables should explain and explore features that are material to the evaluative questions at hand. They should aim to get to the point and to illustrate the point vividly.
- **Intelligible.** The prose of parables should avoid boilerplate yet be understandable at the level of everyday language. A parable should be simple, direct and credible (see Chapter Five, 'The Language of Value'.)

Three extended parables of value structure the middle chapters of this book, and there are shorter ones throughout. It is important to reiterate that a parable of value is a dynamic set of writing principles, not a template to be copied.

If you are an artist or cultural organisation, you might think of a case that reflects your core purpose. What is it like to talk about the experiences you actually create, rather than provide a shopping list of all imaginable positive outcomes 'in the language of government'?

CHAPTER TWO

Parable of Value 1: Patrick White and the Problem of Numbers

In the sketch comedy program *That Mitchell and Webb Look*, two contestants on a spoof TV quiz show call out random numbers in response to other numbers displayed on a coloured board. Periodically, and for no apparent reason, they are told by the show host, 'that's numberwang!', and everyone reacts as if the right answer had been given.[24] It's funny because today numbers really do seem to have a life of their own, appearing as evidence for any and all arguments, illustrating no-see-ums, like fluctuations in the global economy or rises in the average body mass index. Economic statistics, sporting statistics, health statistics, education statistics, and, of course, cultural statistics: using numbers as a guide to public perceptions and policy making is of comparatively recent origin, yet it is an approach that has taken deep root. The reason for it is not hard to fathom. As social life becomes more complex, relying on methods of resource allocation and means of communication distant from the coalface of lived experience, the problem of 'imperative coordination', as the sociologist Max Weber called it, has grown forbiddingly dense.[25]

---

24 David Mitchell and Robert Webb, *That Mitchell and Webb Look*: thatmitchellandwebb.wikia.com/wiki/Numberwang.

25 Max Weber, *The Theory of Social and Economic Organisation*. Translated and edited by Talcott Parsons (London: Free Press of Glencoe, 1947).

Yet even as computers generate floods of data, the human brain remains much as evolution made it 50,000 years ago. Data has to be cognitively processed and interpreted in ways that are valid not only statistically, but which ensure the context and underlying assumptions are properly represented. As Daniel Kahneman and Amos Tversky's celebrated research on decision-making shows, this is harder than we imagine.[26] Most of what we do is 'thinking fast', using instinct and shortcuts to leap to conclusions that let us move on to the next thing. We look out the window, see blue sky, and leave home without our raincoat. Careful analysis of the Bureau of Meteorology website might lead to the same conclusion, but might also make us late for work. 'Thinking slow' is arduous and our brains do their best to avoid it. Kahneman comments:

> I propose a simple account of how we generate intuitive opinions on complex matters. If a satisfactory answer to a hard question is not found quickly, System 1 [i.e. thinking fast] will find a related question that is easier and will answer it. I call the operation of answering one question in place of another *substitution*.[27]

Numbers can be a tool for hard thinking. But they can also provide a reductive proxy to avoid difficult decisions. Is a theatre company in regional Australia, with a distinct context and purpose, good enough to retain public funding? With numbers, it is important to acknowledge, there is *always* a context and *always* a set of assumptions. But neither context nor assumptions are typically visible in a set of numbers. They have to be made to speak, and this is the job of the accompanying words which we are inclined to believe are less 'objective' in their demonstrative prowess. The

---

26 These ideas are most accessible in Daniel Kahneman, *Thinking, Fast and Slow* (London: Allen Lane, 2011).

27 Kahneman, *Thinking, Fast and Slow*, 97.

message may be explicit, but often it is a whispered subtext sitting below collective consciousness, investing seemingly standalone figures with sense. In certain areas, the alignment between words and numbers is tight and that investment uncontentious. A classic example is births, deaths and marriages statistics. In other domains the alignment is looser, especially where the numbers are generated from surveys or samples rather than item-by-item counting. Nearly every opinion poll got the results of the 2016 US Presidential election and the UK Brexit referendum wrong, for reasons that involve a revealing combination of human and methodological error. In a world awash with quantitative data, it is easy to drift from talking about a phenomenon that can be enumerated unequivocally (the birth of an individual) to a phenomenon that can't (the 'birth' of a political movement). Unless the relationship between numbers and things is calibrated, the danger of misleading quantification is high (William Reichman dubbed this 'statistic-u-lation').[28] We get the look of proof rather than its reality, the laundering of assumptions as facts. Numbers are not to blame. The problem lies in our desire to use them as a shortcut for the time-consuming task of acquiring expertise – to substitute numerals for knowledge. In the end, words and numbers are complements. Stories without statistics run the danger of being unrepresentative. Statistics without stories run the danger of being meaningless and decontextualised: of being numberwang.

A Thought Experiment

Imagine a simplified cultural universe in which only three things exist: one book, one reader, and one coin. The reader pays the coin for the book – ignore the problem of who to just for the moment

---

28   W. Reichmann, *Use and abuse of statistics* (New York: Oxford University Press, 1962).

– and reads it. In so doing, the reader engages in an act of exchange. This can be stated thus:

1 coin $\Rightarrow$ 1 book $\Rightarrow$ 1 reader

where '$\Rightarrow$' stands for 'gets entangled with' (or similar phrase).

Three numbers now stand in a complex interrelationship. Books, coins and people are different things. They have different properties and uses. The words in the formula tell us that. The numbers do not. But the numbers provide an equivalential logic that validates the exchange by subsuming book, coin and reader in an all-encompassing order of value. Value is a relation, permitting things to be conjoined that would otherwise be radically distinct. The value relation is a triangle whose corners are an object, a subject, and a measure of equivalence. Remove one of these and the relation collapses. An object without a subject is inert. An object without a measure of equivalence has no means of exchange. And a subject without an object has nothing to value. $1 \Rightarrow 1 \Rightarrow 1$ is thus the configuration of *any* value relation. Value isn't a gumball that comes out of a mental dispenser when you twist a numerical lever. It is an action of conferral, dynamic and human. We might say that value doesn't exist, only *evaluation* exists, the act by which we come into a value relation with the world around us, and engage in it via a means of exchange, be that banknotes, bottle-tops or bitcoins.

How does a reader derive value from their book? How do value relations work? Interesting question! Imagine the following:

1. The reader gets immediate conscious enjoyment, information, or improvement from reading the book – they like it.

2. The reader gets immediate *un*conscious enjoyment, information, or improvement from reading the book – it helps
   them understand something about the world.

3. The reader gets delayed conscious enjoyment, information,
   or improvement from reading the book – later in life it
   helps them reflect on their own personal development.

4. The reader gets delayed *un*conscious enjoyment, information, or improvement from reading the book – the book
   becomes part of their mental furniture.

5. The reader derives an incidental benefit from the book not
   related to the experience of reading it – a stranger spots
   them reading it and strikes up a conversation that leads to
   a friendship.

This list can be extended as we imagine different relations between
subject and object. What about books we dislike but which leave
an impression on us, like Arnold Schwarzenegger's page-turner
memoir *Total Recall*, which the *Guardian* newspaper called 'the
most unpleasant celebrity memoir ever'? [29] Or books that challenge
conventional taste and expectations, like Brett Easton Ellis's
American Psycho or Helen Garner's *Monkey Grip*? Or books that we
read only in part, like the Bible or James Joyce's *Finnegan's Wake*?
Not everything we choose to read is easily enjoyable, and some
books remain arduous to the end. These present the challenge of
saying what other route value takes.

Another set of problems relate to time. Value is a function of time
because evaluation is an act that occurs in time, and *when* it occurs
alters the degree and sometimes the nature of the value relation.
Books we like when were young we may not like when we are older,

---

29 'Arnold Schwarzenegger's autobiography'. Guardian, 4 October, 2012.

and vice versa. Or we can have variable views about a book, liking it one year, indifferent to it the next, then liking it again. Behavioural economists call this 'dynamic inconsistency' or 'time inconsistency'. Our nutritional needs are stable (2,200–2,700 calories a day), as are our sleep requirements (7–9 hours per night). In contrast, our cultural needs are so changeable that even to speak of 'needs' seems a misnomer, until we remember there has been no society in human history without a culture, so it is clearly a constant of some kind.[30]

What about books that become part of the structure of a reader's mind? People often confuse 'subjective' with 'subjectively processed'. The difference is key. There are things that exist only as part of our inner reality. Love, for example, or friendship; suffering; understanding; self-knowledge. These are internally realised, if externally manifested. That doesn't make them arbitrary. Though personal experience is a realm disclosed to each individually, individuals spend a good deal of their lives communicating what it is like, and bringing their perceptions into alignment with those around them. These perceptions aren't relative except in the trivial sense of the word. They are relational, which means that, as John Donne famously observed, no-one 'is an island, entire of itself'.[31] People are joined by myriad inter-subjective bridges that build a sense of community and belonging. Some books contribute significantly to this architecture of connection. Robert Darnton shows how the writing of Rousseau furnished a vocabulary of sense and feeling for Assembly representatives in post-revolutionary

---

30 For a path into this huge territory, see Denis Dutton, *The Art Instinct: Beauty, Pleasure, & Human Evolution* (New York: Bloomsbury Press, 2009); and Brian Boyd, *On the Origin of Stories: Evolution, Cognition, and Fiction* (Cambridge, Mass: Belknap Press of Harvard University Press, 2009).

31 John Donne, *Devotions on Emergent Occasions* (1624), Devotion 17: ebooks. adelaide.edu.au/d/donne/john/devotions/chapter17.html.

France.[32] Isaiah Berlin describes how Russian novels in the nineteenth century operated as a political outlet for the country's oppressed intelligentsia.[33] After World War II, writers like V.S. Naipaul and Chinua Achebe did as much as politicians to shape the thinking of postcolonial nations. Meanwhile, the rise of feminism in the West saw artists and activists working in tandem – often, as with Simone De Beauvoir and Toni Morrison, in the same body – to drive social transformation. In each of these cases, books played a constitutive role in public consciousness and it is impossible to ask what their *value* is without looking at the *values* they embody, an examination that makes the first question meaningful. Evaluation is a whole act, involving our moral, political and aesthetic judgment simultaneously.

This value is easily recognised, but how do you *measure* it? If culture's changeable nature and impact defies easy description, how can it be subjected to a semantically parsimonious 'rule of the count'?

Time, Value and the Drama of Patrick White

Look at three sets of numbers, laid out below in table form:

Table 1

795-16-0	1113-8-6	1069-13-6	1180-6-0
149-1-10	224-15-0	142-13-0	123-3-6

---

32   Robert Darnton, *The Great Cat Massacre and Other episodes in French Cultural History* (New York: Vintage Books, 1985).

33   Isaiah Berlin, *Russian Thinkers* (London: Hogarth Press, 1978).

Table 2

0	0	0	1	0	0	0	0	0	0	0	0	0
0	0	0	0	0	0	0	0	0	0	0	0	0
0	0	0	0	0	0	0	0	0	0	0	0	0
0	0	0	0	1	0	0	0	0	0	0	0	0
0	0	0	0	0	0	0	0	0	0	0	0	0
0	1	2	0	0	0	0	0	1	1	0	0	0
0	0	2	1	1	0	0	0	0	1	0	0	0
0	0	0	0	0	0	1	0	0	0	0	0	0
0	0	0	0	1	1	0	0	0	0	0	1	0
0	0	0	0	0	0	0	0	0	0	1	1	0
0	0	0	0	0	0	0	0	0	0	0	0	0
0	0	0	0	0	0	0	0	0	1	2	0	2
0	0	0	0	0	0	0	0	0	0	0	0	0
0	0	0	2	0	0	0	0	0	0	0	1	0

Table 3

270	343	390	404	382	401	398	366	441	412	353	337	319
76	131	110	132	98	136	171	122	155	156	92	79	130
411	377	333	456	414	534	527	850	836	933	772	294	358
156	112	123	157	177	208	199	451	494	604	499	138	178

What do these figures mean? Without contextual knowledge, you can have no idea. For a start, you would need to know the categories to which they belong. This is another thing to observe about numbers, that in contrast to verbal terms they offer no immediate associations. They 'anchor' on just themselves, large or small only by comparison to other numbers. What their differences signify, or whether they signify anything at all, can only be established by an act of interpretation. This fills otherwise empty figures with significance and illuminates the purpose of generating quantitative data in the first place. Unlike numberwang, numbers in the real world must have a reason for being. This may seem a straightforward observation, but it is not. As the philosopher Eran Tal comments,

> A measurement scale is a mapping – a *homomorphism* – from an empirical to a numerical relational structure, and measurement is the construction of scales. Each type of scale is associated with a set of assumptions or 'axioms' about the qualitative relations obtaining among empirical objects ... A measurement outcome is thus a *region* in parameter space where the relevant theory locates the actual state of the object on the basis of the indications of an instrument. Such a region is considered an adequate representation of the object *only when the theory provides a coherent story* of the ways in which possible indications of the apparatus reflect possible states of the object.[34]

Narrative is the only structure capable of meaningfully linking quantitative mark with qualitative relation. This linking is easy to fudge, fumble or manipulate, because numbers look so precise, pristine, and real world phenomena so clearly are not. For numbers to be of use, then, they need proper anchors in the real world so that mathematical representation is valid, readable and ethical. We don't count the hairs on the back of our heads because there would be no point. We don't measure the love we have for our children because a metric would be questionable. Our sense of value *precedes* the act of measurement. Things aren't of value because we count them. We count them because we believe they are of value.

---

34 Eran Tal, 'Old and New Problems in Philosophy of Measurement', *Philosophy Compass*, 8/12 (2013), 1159–1173, emphasis added.

Narrative need not be a whole story, but can be a fragment of a story, or even a single word. A prior sense of value brings with it metaphors that categorise activities in an understandable way. 'Arts and crafts', 'the cultural industries', 'the creative industries', 'heritage', 'the creative economy': all these are *stories* subsuming different activities under a common name. Typically, we are unaware of the consequences of this when we stare at a list of numbers. Yet calling something 'an industry' or 'a profession' or 'a leisure pursuit' is a nominative act of great rhetorical force. It does more than describe something. It hails it into being. This is hardly a great insight, and yet it is almost always forgotten in the policy-making fray because questioning narratives is an arduous process whereas taking in quantitative data is the work of a moment. The task of evaluation, therefore, *involves* numbers but not in a summative way. To be effective, they need to be fit for purpose (in the current phrase) and validly interpreted. This activity is not a pseudo-scientific demonstration but a careful attention to the way numbers are used and the categories that order them: in short, their narrative potential. To see this in action, let's take a concrete example: the drama of Patrick White.

David Marr tells the story of White and the critic Geoffrey Dutton meeting in Sydney on 24 August 1960:

> Dutton has been commissioned to write a little booklet
> about White for the Lansdowne Press. But he had
> come over to Sydney with another more urgent mission.
> Adelaide's answer to the Edinburgh Festival was after a
> new Australian play. The inaugural festival had seen Alan
> Seymour's *The One Day of the Year* rejected by the governors
> for casting a slur on the fine men who had gone abroad to
> fight in the war. Now a rather desperate hunt was being
> conducted by the festival's drama committee to find a fresh
> Australian play for the second festival in 1962. Dutton's real

mission in Sydney was to winkle out of White a copy of a play he had mentioned a couple of years before.[35]

By 1960 White was a famous novelist with an international reputation. He had also written a play, *The Ham Funeral*, in 1947, which Dutton persuaded him to submit to the drama committee of the Adelaide Festival. The committee unanimously recommended it for production the following year. Thus began for White a journey of calumny and persecution through Australian theatre, a *via dolorosa* many writers have tramped, but perhaps not one so supremely out of joint with the times and audience tastes. Between 1961 and 1965, White wrote three more plays, *Season at Sarsaparilla*, *A Cheery Soul* and *Night on Bald Mountain*, all of which now hold high places in the canon of Australian drama and are regularly lauded. In the 1960s they were very controversial, and White's techniques as a dramatist – surreal and fragmented characterisation, multiple plot lines, heavily symbolic dialogue – were greeted with a mixture of bewilderment, repugnance and condescension.

In 1961, *The Ham Funeral* was forced out of the Adelaide Festival program by its conservative governors, who manipulated the programming committee to get their way. A young medical student, Harry Medlin, the progressively-minded producer of the Adelaide University Theatre Guild (AUTG), staged it, and scheduled *Sarsaparilla* for the following year. These were both semi-amateur productions, however, and the issue of their professional presentation remained unresolved. In the first few months of 1962, John Sumner, the Artistic Director of the Union Theatre Repertory Company (UTRC, now the Melbourne Theatre Company) began a correspondence with White that led to the professional production of *Sarsaparilla* in Melbourne a few months after the AUTG. Table

---

35 David Marr, '"So Much of Our Life in It". Arrogant Adelaide and the Theatre of Patrick White', *Australian Book Review*, May 2012, 12–17.

1 shows the box office receipts from the UTRC season,[36] and even from this slender historical fragment it is possible to see that far from the figures 'speaking for themselves' they frame a complex web of expectations, dispositions, and ingrained behaviour that demands careful interpretation.

Oddly to our eye, there are three sets of digits in each field. That's because these numbers denote Australian currency pre-decimalisation, that is, pounds, shillings and pence. The UTRC ran *Sarsaparilla* for four weeks, a recent change for a company that since its establishment in 1952 had usually offered two or three-week seasons. The figures indicate greater ambition, greater security, or both. The top row shows single ticket purchases, the bottom subscription purchases. Subscription tickets are sold ahead of time: quarterly, biannually or annually. As a theatre production doesn't physically exist at this juncture, what the subscriber actually buys is reputation and promised return: in other words, risk. For single-ticket buyers, by contrast, a show not only exists but has proxies of value that can be readily consulted: critical reviews, media interviews, word of mouth, etc. Risk still exists, but is considerably less. Thus, although the top and bottom row of figures appear to indicate only different points of sale, they actually represent two different evaluative strategies.

Sarsaparilla went quite well at the UTRC, as suggested by the fact that single tickets are five times higher than subscription purchases. This was considered important enough information to be communicated to White's agent, Curtis Brown. The way in which numbers are broken into smaller numbers, the way they are subdivided, totalled and transformed, tells us a great deal about Tal's 'coherent story' that quantitative data is mobilised for. In this case, there are three potential narratives to give the figures

---

36   In author Julian Meyrick's personal possession.

meaning. There is the story of a small, semi-commercial theatre struggling to stay profitable – a task perhaps not so arduous as it had been 10 years earlier, but still difficult. There is the story of a city developing a theatre subscription audience – though judging by the comparative smallness of the numbers, this a slow process. And there is the story of a modernist playwright parading his confronting wares in a professional theatre for the first time. The result is numerically positive. The author's royalty was 10 per cent of total box office receipts: £479-17-6.[37]

It was the most White's drama was destined to earn him that decade. The following year, the UTRC staged *A Cheery Soul,* and royalties were just £174-11-2. The box office statement is not on file, but we can infer, with total income at £1,745-11-8 and assuming the same number of subscription purchases as *Sarsaparilla,* that the ratio of single ticket buyers slipped from 5 to 1 to 3 to 1. Knowing what we know about the subscription vs single ticket narrative, we can further guess that press coverage and word of mouth was poor. The figure of £479-17-6 was a good number for White, £174-11-2 a bad one.

But what does this say about the *value* of *Sarsaparilla* and *A Cheery Soul?* Going from a measure of frequency to a judgment of quality is one of the enticing leaps numbers invite you to make. The more people pay to see something, the more valuable it is, you are inclined to believe. But be wary. Quantitative data tells nothing qualitative unless narrative assumptions are plugged into them. The chosen proxy – in this case, ticket sales – may not be a good indicator of value. Even if it is, its interval or scale may be misleading about degrees of value. A theatre show priced at £1 a seat is not half as

37   This sum can be usefully compared to the minimum male annual wage at the time of £950; see Australian Bureau of Statistics, *The Year Book Australia 1962,* 404: www.abs.gov.au/AUSSTATS/abs@.nsf/allprimarymainfeatures/75BA8D2 1EF7BFA92CA2573AE00045CC6.

good as one priced at £2, and it is nonsense to suggest it. Numbers may work well on one level of explanation but not on another. Low figures for one White drama can be the occasion for one kind of qualitative hypothesis – perhaps the play or the production was not very good. Low figures for White's body of work is the occasion for another – perhaps Australia has trouble understanding its own playwrights. Numbers aggregate, narratives elucidate. Because numbers occupy a thin descriptive air – are a mark without further associations – the transformations they can be subjected to are limitless. This is not true of the things to which they refer. Adding together the box office income of all productions of White plays doesn't tell much about their overall value. If it isn't meaningless, it is of very limited explanatory power because the context in which each play was produced varied so radically.

Table 2, which looks a bit like an old-fashioned computer punch card, shows the number of professional productions of White's plays from 1960 to 1985.[38] There are more zeros in the table than any other kind of number. Absence is a type of presence, as Arab mathematicians discerned; the number zero itself is the result of a qualitative insight. From 1961 to 1964, White's plays attracted 10 productions. Thereafter – despite the prominence of White as a Nobel Prize winner in 1973 – productions were few and far between until 1976, when he received two in one year. From 1976 to 1985, there are no less than 13 productions of White plays. What was going on?

Again, numbers do not tell the story; the story gives sense to the numbers. In 1976, a close relationship between White and the

---

38 These figures are taken from the AusStage database. Great care is taken to ensure that the information entered into AusStage is correct. However, while its dataset is extensive, it is not yet comprehensive. Though the figures in the section have been checked a number of times, small errors are still possible, and this should be borne in mind in respect of their interpretation.

director Jim Sharman led to a revival of *Sarsaparilla* by the Old Tote Theatre (the predecessor of the Sydney Theatre Company). Designed by Brian Thomson and showing all the panache of the Australian 'New Wave' theatrical imagination, its unprecedented critical and popular success indicates a cultural transformation. In 1963, the critic Frank Harris dismissed *Sarsaparilla* as

> a parade of puppets. The yapping of the dogs ... sounded like a bad ... joke; the chorus of derision against the false gentility and cliché-ridden lives of the neighbouring Pogson and Knott families became tiresome; even the two little girls who learn the facts of life by watching the dog pack... are ... a weak stage device.[39]

But in 1976 the critic Geraldine Pascal greeted it as

> something rich and strange and exciting ... that ... may point to a growing maturity in Australian theatre and, if accepted, a critical self-confidence in our audience. In the razzle-dazzle of time and motion since the play was written in 1961 ... it gained an odd, if not controversial reputation for being difficult, abstrusely expressionist, and as a cold, clinical vivisection of Australian life. Well, expressionist may be the right label ... but *Sarsaparilla* is a rich, sympathetic, complex play... We may have grown up enough in the past fourteen years to accept White's vision.[40]

One day top rooster, next day feather duster. Or in White's case, the other way round. Theatre is fertile ground for such volte-faces, 180-degree switches in social estimations of value. There is no doubt that in the 1960s Patrick White was regarded by all but a

---

39   Frank Harris, 'Cut the Cackle, Mr. Tasker', *Sydney Morning Herald*, 23 May 1963.
40   Geraldine Pascall, 'A Welcome Season', *The Australian*, 8 November 1978.

small coterie of admirers as a failed dramatist. *Sarsaparilla, Ham Funeral, A Cheery Soul* and *Night on Bald Mountain* were discussed, in large part, as technically flawed and morally distasteful. If the theatre-going public in Australia in the 1960s could be said to have a collective skin, White's plays made that skin crawl. In the 1970s, the situation was entirely different. Not only did the reputation of his original four dramas undergo rehabilitation, but he started writing new plays – in 1978 *Big Toys,* in 1982 *Signal Driver,* in 1983 *Netherwood,* in 1987 *Shepherd on the Rocks. Signal Driver* was staged for the Adelaide Festival. Twenty-five years after having been forced out of its program, he was welcomed back as a lead attraction.

The zeros in Table 2 are an eloquent absence if, and *only* if, the right questions are asked. Once more a number of narrative pathways are available. One story is that of a would-be playwright struggling with rejection and neglect, then rediscovery and endorsement. Another is that of a theatre audience bewildered by modernist drama who learn to understand it. A third is the story of a new level of skill among Australian theatre artists, a profession now with the talent and experience to stage winning productions of White's difficult plays.

When we overlay Table 1 with Table 2 these narratives emerge in full. Qualitative meaning and quantitative mark come together in a structural relation that historian Alun Munslowe calls 'narrative supervenience'.[41] The basic unit is the individual production of the individual play. Without these, there is no concept of White's 'body of work' to refer to. Yet while the numbers get bigger, their interpretation demands that we keep different narrative perspectives separate. You have to look down on numbers from a higher point of understanding, and 'run' them towards this point to see what they

---

41   Alun Munslow, *Narrative and History* (Basingstoke: Palgrave Macmillan, 2007, 83).

indicate. To reduce a theatre season to a set of audience numbers is like reducing a football season to its final ladder.

Table 3 provides the big picture.[42] The time period is the same as Table 2, 1960 to 1983. The top row shows professional productions of overseas plays in Australia, the bottom row professional productions of Australian ones. The latter climb dramatically from 1976 to 1985 before dropping back to 1960s levels in 1984 and 1985. White's story is part of the story of Australian drama, and this narrative in turn relies on what happened to White to give it meaning and shape. We can generalise the White narrative, use it as a case study. But we can't aggregate it without doing damage to a causal analysis. Was the 1976 production of *Sarsaparilla* a turning point for Australian theatre, a moment of national self-confidence? Or was it a consequence of it? What's the story? Is it one of modernism finally arriving in Australian theatre? Or Australian plays, including modernist ones, finally arriving in Australian theatre programs? Or is it the appearance of the so-called 'new audience'? Did a renovated public provide a new reception for this drama because White's *values* – sharp, literary, both loving and hating Australian life and mores – no longer blocked perception of their *value*?

Here are the tables with their categories attached, available for narrative interpretation because there is now the contextual knowledge to handle it. Note however, that this is hard work and doesn't generate a simple conclusion:

Table 1: 'The Season at Sarsaparilla' UTRC 1962. Box office summary

	Week 1	Week 2	Week 3	Week 4	Totals
	£. s. d	£. s. d	£. s. d	£. s. d	£. s. d
Subscribers	795-16-0	1113-8-6	1069-13-6	1180-6-0	639-13-4
Gen. Public	149-1-10	224-15-0	142-13-0	123-3-6	4798-17-4
Totals	944-17-10	133-3-6	1212-6-6	1303-9-6	4798-17-4

---

42   These figures are also taken from the AusStage database.

Table 2: Professional production of plays by Patrick White, by year, 1960–1985

	1960	1961	1962	1963	1964	1965	1966	1967	1968	1969	1970	1971	1972
A Cheery Soul	0	0	0	1	0	0	0	0	0	0	0	0	0
Big Toys	0	0	0	0	0	0	0	0	0	0	0	0	0
Netherwood	0	0	0	0	0	0	0	0	0	0	0	0	0
Bald Mountain	0	0	0	0	1	0	0	0	0	0	0	0	0
Signal Driver	0	0	0	0	0	0	0	0	0	0	0	0	0
Ham Funeral	0	1	2	0	0	0	0	0	1	1	0	0	0
Sarsaparilla	0	0	2	1	1	0	0	0	0	1	0	0	0
Totals	0	1	4	2	2	0	0	0	1	2	0	0	0

	1973	1974	1975	1976	1977	1978	1979	1980	1981	1982	1983	1984	1985
A Cheery Soul	0	0	0	0	0	0	1	0	0	0	0	0	0
Big Toys	0	0	0	0	1	1	0	0	0	0	0	1	0
Netherwood	0	0	0	0	0	0	0	0	0	0	1	1	0
Bald Mountain	0	0	0	0	0	0	0	0	0	0	0	0	0
Signal Driver	0	0	0	0	0	0	0	0	0	1	2	0	2
Ham Funeral	0	0	0	0	0	0	0	0	0	0	0	0	0
Sarsaparilla	0	0	0	2	0	0	0	0	0	0	0	1	0
Totals	0	0	0	2	1	1	1	0	0	1	3	3	2

Only when you know the story of numbers can you judge the linking of quantitative indicator to qualitative relation. Value is not well behaved. Assessors slide from proxy to narrative without being aware of it, the meaning of numbers in the whispered subtext they carry around in their heads. The further removed evaluation gets from lived cultural experience, the less likely quantified data is to represent it well. Costs, prices, attendances, sales, 'footfalls', 'eyeballs on screens', etc. – these countable marks only reflect

Table 3: Totals and percentage of professional productions of overseas and Australian plays in Australia, 1960–1985

	1960	1961	1962	1963	1964	1965	1966	1967	1968	1969	1970	1971	1972
Overseas plays	270	343	390	404	382	401	398	366	441	412	353	337	319
Australian plays	76	131	110	132	98	136	171	122	155	156	92	79	130
% Total	14	17	20	21	19	20	20	19	22	21	18	17	16

	1973	1974	1975	1976	1977	1978	1979	1980	1981	1982	1983	1984	1985
Overseas plays	411	377	333	456	414	534	527	850	836	933	772	294	358
Australian plays	156	112	123	157	177	208	199	451	494	604	499	138	178
% Total	21	19	17	23	21	27	27	43	42	47	39	15	18

increments of value to the degree there is attentiveness to the real experiences they append. Perhaps this is why large-scale projects, such as the opening ceremony of the Sydney Olympic Games in 2000 or the Anzac celebrations of the Gallipoli landings in 2015, go right rather than wrong, satisfying expectations and entailing lively conversations about their value. Public attention is on them, so they can celebrate the nation and criticise the treatment of Indigenous peoples in the same narrative frame.

Evaluations of cultural activities thus happen in multiple ways, rather than massing up, as David Throsby has convincingly argued when talking about the workings of the theatre market.[43] This means assessment processes have to encompass several simultaneous 'value states', somewhat like a quantum computer. The reception of White's plays in the 1960s was not 'wrong'. Perhaps the high position we now give them will be seen as 'wrong' in 50 years' time. One set of value relations does not supplant another. They co-exist. Evaluation strategies have to contend with this irreducible social fact and, to some extent, explain it. Numbers are a good tool for furnishing such explanations. They never provide an explanation in themselves.

---

43 David Throsby, 'Perception of Quality in Demand for Theatre' (1982). Reprinted in *Journal of Cultural Economics* (1990): 14/1.

Box 3 Farnarkulator

It's the Farnarkulator, so named in memory of sports fan and comic genius John Clarke. It's a sophisticated algorithm for assessing quality across the realm of sport. It mines big data in rich and complex ways so that valid comparisons and rankings can be made within and between different sports. No longer will pubs be held hostage to endless disputes about whether Stoke City is better at soccer than the Silver Ferns are at netball. If you pump in the data, you can find out *definitively* whether any modern sportsperson/horse exceeds Don Bradman or Phar Lap in excellence. Governments and advertisers will be grateful for a *quick and easy way* of deciding which team to back with a new stadium, sponsorship, or elite training program.

If you smell a rat, that's because the idea of the Farnarkulator is self-evidently silly, and Laboratory Adelaide has discovered no attempt to do anything like it. Everyone we've talked to is adamant that any index that purports to compare across sports is nonsense. Sport is replete with real numbers that can be aggregated in myriad ways. But they can only shed angled light, at best, on the experience of players and spectators.

There are fewer real numbers in arts and culture than in sport, and they tell us even less about the quality of the experience. The number of notes played in a symphony does not help us distinguish a good one from a bad. Bendigo Art Gallery got sell-out crowds in 2016 for a Marilyn Monroe exhibition, but didn't get similar numbers to 'House of Mirrors' in Rosalind Park the following year. But what does this mean? Audience numbers can inform a judgment of relative success, but they cannot determine it, or future decisions on programming. If regional art galleries put on nothing but fashion blockbusters, something crucial in the art ecology would be broken.

People in the arts are often sitting ducks for big data carpetbaggers, who peddle the promise that, with enough time and effort, a way of avoiding hard, personal, risky choices about comparative value is available.

Used where context is understood, and subject to robust interrogation, numbers can be worth the trouble. However, they can also be a distraction from more important but less measurable purposes, and:

1. They provide little security from external blows, because funding decisions are always political and not *really* based on the sorts of evidence they claim to want.
2. They quickly generate internal targets that work to the metrics and not to reality, so they distort internal practice.
3. If they escape into the public realm, they become targets and rankings in next to no time.
4. And the targets have to be exceeded every year because growth is the constant expectation.

Algorithm is just a fancy word for conceptual gadget. And the gadget for measuring cultural value, an artistic **Farnarkulator**, is not on the horizon.

CHAPTER THREE

Parable of Value 2: Digital Disruption / There's an App for That!

Disruption is a loaded word. But it is also an empty signifier, hollowed out by misuse and overuse, consumed and regurgitated by corporations hungry for the next slick management term. As we go to press, happenings in this field are fluid. It is too soon to tell how the #metoo movement and the 2018 Facebook/Cambridge Analytica data sharing scandal (and the algorithmic reality underpinning it) will affect our lives long-term. *Digital disruption,* however, means something more particular. Wikipedia (a senior member of the Digital Disruptors' Club) says that in the field of business the term refers to 'an innovation that creates a new market and value network and eventually disrupts an existing market and value network, displacing established market leading firms, products and alliances'.[44] The phrase was coined by Clayton Christensen in his 1995 book *The Innovator's Dilemma.* But the term has mutated in usage, as terms tend to do. In the NPR program 'All Things Considered', Kevin Roose points out: 'these days [disruption]'s used to sort of mean cool ... [and] anything that's sort of vaguely new or interesting'.[45] The word 'digital' needs some investigation too. It is just as ubiquitous, if seemingly less controversial.

---

44   'Disruptive Innovation', Wikipedia: en.wikipedia.org/wiki/Disruptive_innovation
45   Audie Cornish, 'The Distracting Problem with the Term "Disruption"'. Interview with Kevin Roose. NPR's 'All Things Considered' program 15

What does 'digital disruption' promise and/or threaten for arts and culture? There are a variety of opinions on this. In the 2016 Brian Johns lecture, Julianne Schultz, one of Australia's leading public intellectuals, called for action to protect Australian culture from a suffocating globalisation driven by digital production, consumption and dissemination mechanisms. For Schultz, in the age of the FAANG (Facebook, Apple, Amazon, Netflix and Google), 'we're all global citizens, which threatens to make national cultural institutions both more vulnerable, but also more important than ever'.[46] For most people, digital disruption refers to the idea that the digital provides new ways of doing things, including cultural things, that upend traditional ways of creating and participating, of making and sharing. Culture was always ripe as a key site for this to occur. Media scholars the world over are busy conceptualising what Netflix means, or Spotify, or Google Books. The shift from consuming single episodes to binge watching, for example, changes the experience of television drama. But digital disruption also changes our understanding of value. Value, it is claimed, is now to be found not so much in the content as in the curation, in the infrastructure that allows for discovering, queuing, sharing and favouriting (an interesting neologism, that one). It's in the convenience, in the way the service fits into our way of life. It's in the *platform*.

December 2014: www.npr.org/2014/12/15/371010839/the-distracting-problem-with-the-term-disruption.

46   Julianne Schultz, 'Australia Must Act Now to Preserve its Culture in the Face of Global Tech Giants', *The Conversation*, 2 May 2016.

Platform versus Stuff

Let's take a quick tour around the major digital disruptors. Netflix originally grew out of a video and DVD postal service. Its catch-phrase was 'no late fines, ever'. Revolutionary for people for whom getting to a video store was a problem. This is a classic fable of modern entrepreneurship and marketing. It addresses a real but relatively minor issue, and wipes out an industry because its service is more convenient to use. A lot of disruption for a little improvement. Now Netflix creates its own original content, using its algorithmic knowledge of viewing habits to direct production budgets. It has sold its services to Australians – once hailed as the biggest illegal downloaders in the world – off the back of the argument that we will be happy to pay for movies and television shows if quick and convenient access is provided to allow equal(ish) participation with US and UK audiences. Netflix uses a collaborative filtering method of generating recommendations, including a star system that asks users to vote on programs in their catalogue. It compares users' viewing histories to predict the percentage likelihood a user will enjoy a particular title, offering recommendations filtered for recency and other less visible factors, such as which titles they are actively promoting. David Beer calls an algorithm the 'decision-making parts of code' and in that way they clearly have an inherent power to manipulate.[47]

Spotify, the music streaming service, grew out of a response to file-sharing practices, capitalising on the early failure of the less-than-legal Napster, established in 1999 as a peer-to-peer file-sharing platform. Where Napster had no connection with the artists whose work it distributed, Spotify paid royalties to its musicians, albeit insultingly low ones. Music lovers rejoiced to find a convenient and

---

47   David Beer, 'The Social Power of Algorithms', *Information, Communication &*
       Society, 20.1 (2017), 5.

responsible way to listen to old favourites and discover new ones. For many of its users, it is Spotify's recommendation engine that makes the subscription fee attractive. Again, this engine employs algorithms that note what you are adding to your playlists, what you are listening to and, crucially, what you are skipping over, to shape a suite of 30 new songs, a customised mixtape 'for your listening pleasure', once a week.

There are many different versions of recommendation engines, employing different approaches to the 'value-add' role of curation or discovery. Think about Amazon's prompt: 'people who bought this also bought …'. Sometimes it's useful, sometimes it's hilariously dumb. It's a crude system relying on the punt that similar-seeming customers will have similar interests. When Spotify's metadata style guide was leaked in 2015,[48] it revealed the usual technical advice: how to deal with different or non-standard spellings of a name; how to account for creative roles (including producer and lyricists, as well as performing artists); the problem of remastered releases; the categorical distinction between a single, an EP, an album, a compilation; and so on. But in doing so it also released a lot of less innocent information about their techniques for generating recommendation lists.

Pandora is Spotify's best-known antecedent, though there is also Last.fm, and Apple Music is currently seeking a stronger market foothold. Pandora's curation depends on tagging music by attributes. Its Music Genome Project 'captures the essence of music' by reducing music to 450 attributes, or 'genes', via an in-house team of musicologists.[49] These musicologists listen to 20–40 seconds of a

---

48 Spotify Metadata Style Guide Version 2, September 2015. As leaked on the website DailyRindBlog: www.dailyrindblog.com/newsletter/ SpotifyMetadataStyleGuideV1.pdf.

49 This, in contrast to crowd-sourced attribute tagging or folksonomies. See Tim Westergren, 'The Music Genome Project': pandora.com/mgp (2007).

song then attach metadata, a list of relevant attributes, to classify it. Sub-genomes determine the fields to be populated (a folk music song will generate a different set of possibilities to swing or heavy metal). The attributes count some things that can be measured precisely: beats per minutes, use of particular harmonies or instruments, etc. Other traits are less objective, such as 'musical influence' or how dominant a rhythm is or the intensity of a track. There is training for this, calibration, peer review. But in the end it is what it appears to be: personal judgment.

This inevitable subjectivity raises inevitable questions about partiality. Why do women artists appear less frequently than men in the recommendation list? Are the reasons for this systemic or cultural? Is it because fewer women are played on the radio or get recording contracts, so fewer women appear in self-generated playlists, so fewer women appear in recommendation lists? One of Laboratory Adelaide's research team tried to alter this, by adding only women artists for several weeks in a row, thus expressing a clear musical preference. But it didn't have much effect on the recommendations arriving in the playlist each Monday morning.

Recommendation engines tend to be opaque for commercial reasons, which means that even though we know the result, we can't discover what drives the choices.[50] The engine in Spotify is a big data project that depends on and deploys our 'taste profiles', generated from our listening habits. These are correlated with the more than two billion playlists generated by its 140 million people, of which 70 million are paying users.[51] The Spotify team has made some of its technical information available through a Slide Share

---

50 On the socially retrograde consequences of this 'black box' tendency among algorithms, see Cathy O'Neil, *Weapons of Math Destruction*.

51 As of January 2018 (data from the Spotify website).

presentation, 'From Idea to Execution: Spotify's Discover Weekly'.[52] According to this inside information, the big data of users' playlists is then processed using collaborative filtering and natural language processing. Spotify treats a playlist as a document, and the songs in a playlist as words, and their team uses commonly available text mining tools to drill deep into the data.

Like Netflix, Spotify uses curation as a 'value-add'. Users can both access and discover content through their services and the big data algorithms developed behind the scenes. Value in this context is conditional to the key terms applied to discover it, and the tail of metadata inevitably wags the dog of content. What needs to be much better understood, therefore, is the decisive impact of this hidden curation on our actual cultural experience.

---

52   Chris Johnson, Engineering Manager, Recommendations and Personalization, Spotify 'Discover: From Idea to Execution: Spotify's Discover Weekly'. Published 16 November 2015: www.slideshare.net/MrChrisJohnson/from-idea-to-execution-spotifys-discover-weekly/5-Discover.

Box 4 The Politics of Metadata, Tully's Experience

A few years ago, I worked as an indexer for AustLit, the Australian Literature Resource. This is a digital database of literature written in Australia or by Australians. For an online project, it has great longitudinal credibility. It was established in 2000 by combining a number of disparate literature databases around the nation. Between 2008 and 2013, I spent some hours a week contributing to the big task of keeping AustLit up to date by adding newly published works and plugging gaps in its historical content. 'Adding in' a new published work meant starting a new record in the database and entering the standard bibliographic attributes: title, author, publisher, place of publication, date of publication, and so on; but then also contributing some subject-content indexing: that is, key terms to indicate what a particular work was about.

This last step is the crucial one. Subject-content indexing means that anyone looking up works about, say, FJ Holdens, or lesbian relationships, or Uluru, can find the range of texts (novels/poems/ short stories) that contain the themes and content they are looking for. There is a list of key indexing terms that can be added to a record, provided as a thesaurus. New terms can be used, but only if really needed. Too many key terms in the thesaurus make the search exercise less useful because it doesn't connect like with like. It's too specific. Someone researching pythons in literature may or may not be interested in the broader question of snakes, or the Rainbow Serpent, or lizards. The trick is to create a record for a text so it is as discoverable as possible without appearing too often as a false positive.

When I began this indexing work, it was slow going. I would agonise over every poem. What did it *mean*? What did the author *intend*? How could it be appropriately situated in the vast field of Australian literature? After a while, my indexing speed increased. I got more efficient, pumping my way through book after book of poetry. I congratulated myself on my skills. But this newfound speed had a darker side. I was reading and interpreting the texts according to the structure of the database and its thesaurus of key terms. Many poems became about 'conflict in relationships' or 'growing up' or 'spiritual journeying'. The act of interpretation – the value-add – was outsourced to a series of murky and often contested metadata categories. What does this tell us about the way that we make decisions about content, value and relevance in arts and culture in digital environments every day? Metadata is an informational structure. Even when completely accurate, metadata is political. Informational structures and infrastructures directly influence the work people do inside them.

Think, for example, about the 2015 controversy over Google's image-recognition algorithm that auto-tagged pictures of black people as 'gorillas'. Or Microsoft's 2016 AI chatbot Tay, sent into Twitter to chat with real people and learn from them. Microsoft had to hit the kill switch within 24 hours because Tay fell began tweeting racist, anti-Semitic, sexist and transphobic comments. It had learned not how to be convincingly human, but how to dehumanise others, spewing back content derived from what people were saying to it. Politicians often swallow the utopian claims of digital technology while only being dimly aware of how it actually *works*. In a 2014 interview with David Spears on Sky News, George Brandis, then Attorney General as well as Arts Minister, clearly demonstrated that he didn't understand the concept of metadata, or how it can give information away.[53] And yet it was central to the laws on mandatory data retention he was trying to introduce.

Government is a latecomer to algorithmic supervision and control, though, if the Cambridge Analytica scandal is anything to go by, it is a superuser of algorithmic practices for instrumental ends. Other players have been working in the space for a long time. Just as Spotify looks at what you play and what you skip to determine the difference between what you say you like (songs you save to your playlist) and what you really like (songs you play in their entirety or repeatedly), Amazon collects data on what, how fast, and how much you read on your Kindle and sells the data on.[54] An author may have a bestselling book but if the data collected shows that readers don't finish it there is unlikely to be a market for a follow-up. This is useful business information for publishers. Amazon sells it to them. Where is the boundary between the optimisation of investment and customer demand on the one hand and the place of

---

53   See 'David Speers – PM Agenda', Sky News. Uploaded 13 October 2014, YouTube: www.youtube.com/watch?v=HGURYRjEiRI.

54   Alison Flood, 'Big E-reader is Watching You', *The Guardian*, 4 July 2012.

literary judgment and longitudinal value (value that develops over a longer time period)? Inevitably the practice of making publishing decisions based on e-reader data shapes the future literary record. Did Eliot's publishers survey her readers on their preferred book length before printing *Middlemarch*? There are privacy concerns inherent in this new situation too. The Amazon Kindle's 'Notes and Highlights' functions have potential for strong positive pay-offs for reading: they may facilitate different and perhaps deeper kinds of reading across social networks. They may motivate reluctant readers, or support readings in educational settings, or enable guided readings through the involvement of authors themselves. Yet social reading on Kindle also raises concerns about the misuse of deeply networked and commercially-oriented technology for 'black-box' supervision and manipulation of a once private act.[55]

The FAANG tech giants keep their motivations hidden behind a shroud of marketing blather about consumer choice. But utopian and dystopian potentials are never far apart, and examples in the digital realm are not hard to find.

The Google Books project began, according to their own myth of origins, with the dream of its young college creators to have sources at their fingertips:

> In 1996, Google co-founders Sergey Brin and Larry Page were graduate computer science students working on a research project supported by the Stanford Digital Library Technologies Project. Their goal was to make digital libraries work, and their big idea was as follows: in a future world in which vast collections of books are digitized, people would use a 'web crawler' to index the books' content and analyze the connections between them, determining

---

55   See Tully Barnett, 'Social Reading: The Kindle's Social Highlighting Function and Emerging Reading Practices', *Australian Humanities Review* (2014).

any given book's relevance and usefulness by tracking the
number and quality of citations from other books.[56]

To make this dream a reality, in 2002 Google partnered with a
number of prominent university libraries and began digitising
millions of works, shipping some to Mountain View, their
California headquarters, and digitising others onsite at libraries by
bringing in teams and technology to do so. Despite lawsuits from
the Authors' Guild, class actions by publishers, and calls to stop
by eloquent authors such as Ursula Le Guin[57], they steamrolled
ahead.[58] Later Microsoft sought to compete, but by then Google
Books had too much critical mass. Microsoft terminated a planned
project with the British Library, conceding that no-one could take
on Google. Why so much time, effort, lawyers' fees and force of will
to create the Google Books project? There is a simple answer: the
data collected from people's use of these resources help Google sell
targeted advertising. But there is also a more complicated answer:
Google uses the content of books to train artificial intelligence.[59]
Frankenstein's monster learned to behave like a human being by
listening to and then reading literature in Mary Shelley's novel
published two centuries ago. Now AI is reading works of literature
great and small in much the same way.

Google's handling of the Google Arts and Culture Institute
(GACI) is less controversial, but just as instructive in thinking about
the value of culture in digital platforms. January 2018 saw a flurry of

---

56 'Google Books History': www.google.com/intl/en/googlebooks/about/history.
html.

57 Alison Flood, 'Authors Denied Appeal to Stop Google Scanning Books', *The
Guardian*, 20 April 2016.

58 Tully Barnett, 'The Human Trace in Google Books', in *Border Crossings*, edited
by Diana Glenn and Graham Tulloch (Kent Town: Wakefield Press, 2016),
53–71.

59 Richard Lea, 'Google Swallows 11,000 Novels to Improve AI's Conversation',
The Guardian, 28 September 2016.

interest in the Google Arts and Culture app's selfie feature. There is a acrimonious debate over the relationship between selfies and arts and culture. In 2014, the *New Republic*'s Chloe Schama demanded that people 'Stop Taking Selfies in Front of Works of Art!', complete with exclamation mark to drive home her frustration at the advent of 'Museum Selfie Day'.[60] But by 2017, selfies as 'engagement activities' had reached top galleries worldwide. In March 2017, the Saatchi Gallery in London opened its 'Selfie to Self-Expression' exhibition and #SaatchiSelfie competition. Naturally, GACI sought to use selfies to drive engagement with its own platform:

> The Google Arts & Culture platform hosts millions of artifacts and pieces of art, ranging from prehistory to the contemporary, shared by museums across the world. But the prospect of exploring all that art can be daunting. To make it easier, we dreamt up a fun solution: connect people to art by way of a fundamental artistic pursuit, the search for the self ... or, in this case, the selfie.[61]

GACI hadn't made much of a splash until January 2018 when Google introduced a function to enable users to filter cultural artefacts not by year, genre, nationality or location, but by visual similarity to the users themselves. That is, through the app it is now possible to find people in art who look like you. You use the camera to take a photo of yourself and the app identifies artworks that resemble it along with a 'resemblance percentage' score. 'Finding yourself' in art has never been quite so narcissistic. But it is driving up attendances at visual arts events and participation with culture.

Underneath all this lies the same politics of association as the AustLit thesaurus of key terms. It needs careful analysis rather than

---

60   Chloe Schama, 'Stop Taking Selfies in Front of Works of Art!', *The New Republic*, 22 January 2014.
61   Google Arts and Culture website: artsandculture.google.com.

glib enthusiasm, as the rise of Critical Algorithm Studies attests.[62] Ned Rossiter and Soenke Zehle argue that 'algorithmic experience is the new terrain of extractive industries within contemporary capitalism whose structural logic is itself algorithmic'.[63] Put more bluntly: 'the rise of algorithmic architectures' is 'central to the capture of experience'. People need metadata systems and recommendation engines. But they also need to understand the restrictive intellectual and cultural conditions under which they do their work.[64] When a headline passes our screens telling us that 6,000 works of children's literature have just been digitised and made available for free online – an accessibility that is contingent on access to literacy and technology – open-access warriors may leap for joy. But do we open the source? Do we actually *read* them? Rarely. Because 6,000 works is too many. How can we find anything of value even to peruse? As author Neil Gaiman has famously said 'Google can bring you back 100,000 answers. A librarian can bring you back the right one.'[65]

Openness

That skill of finding the right answer, the right book, the right piece of information is even more crucial in the move towards open

62 For more information, see Tarleton Gillespie and Nick Seaver, 'Critical Algorithm Studies: A Reading List', *Socialmediacollective.org* (2016) (socialmediacollective.org/reading-lists/critical-algorithm-studies/) or the special section of *Big Data & Society* on 'Algorithms in Culture': journals. sagepub.com/page/bds/collections/algorithms-in-culture.

63 Ned Rossiter and Soenke Zehle, 'The Aesthetics of Algorithmic Experience', in *The Routledge Companion to Art and Politics*, edited by Randy Martin (London: Routledge, 2015), 214–21.

64 Nick Seaver, 'Algorithms as Culture: Some Tactics for the Ethnography of Algorithmic Systems', *Big Data & Society*, 4.2 (2017).

65 Neil Gaimain, 'Neil Gaiman on Libraries'. YouTube clip on the Library Stuff website, uploaded 20 April 2010: www.librarystuff.net/2010/04/20/neil-gaiman-on-libraries/.

access, open data and big data. These movements are crucial for exposing modern democracy and its governments to public scrutiny. Big data disrupts exponentially. 'Big Data Means Big Disruption', wrote Daniel Newman in *Forbes* in 2014.[66]

The vast majority of research data is created with public money and so there is a strong argument for public access to it. The data opened up might come from science, health, or government itself – a wide variety of different areas. This would allow research collaboration beyond the boundaries of one research team or project, and findings to be available for revision and reuse. So the open data movement is a public good. But it can also be a public relations exercise: the appearance of openness, adhering to few principles of open data in practice. No-one looks at the data, but the (paying) public are comforted by the fact that the research findings are 'out there'.

Quantity can be the enemy of quality, or even of accessibility. Open data can be a means of obfuscation, for 'hiding in plain sight', not by withholding data from public scrutiny but by creating a deluge – by providing more data than can be properly considered, examined, contextualised, or even located. Think of legal dramas, where document deluge in discovery processes is used as a way of overwhelming smaller law firms. 'Give them everything', says the big wig with a malicious sneer.

Open access privileges choice as if it were an innocent and wholly free activity. We all like to think we are choosing. But we often allow ourselves to be herded. Choice is good, but not an absolute good. Some herding occurs through public sentiment, some through metadata (the categories things are put in and the relationships between those categories). Much of it now occurs through algorithms. Search engines appear to be neutral, but the information you are seeking is undiscoverable until a search engine interprets

---

66   Daniel Newman, 'Big Data Means Big Disruption', *Forbes*, 3 June 2014.

your keyword request and lays down a pathway to the content. Few searchers look past the first screen of hits. Advertisements dominate the opening screen that any search engine returns. Search Engine Optimisation can be applied to get your webpage higher up the list of returns but there are limits to the effectiveness of this. Safiya Umoja Noble argues that search engines are definitely not ideologically neutral tools but rather systems, designed by humans embedded in particular power structures. They reflect the problems, assumptions, perspectives and biases of the contexts from which they come, and in which they are complicit.[67]

While open access makes some sense for the results of publically funded research, the case for similarly free 'creative content' is predicated on the false notion that all people in society are equitably rewarded for their work. The consumer expectation that digital stuff should be cheap or free exploits the creators of content who are often artists making a living precariously in the so-called 'gig economy'. The owners of platforms (the tech companies and engineers employed by them) have high salaries and secure employment, even as they use the creative outputs of people expected to provide their labour for free or low prices. They often do, victims of the passion they demonstrate, or are expected to demonstrate, for their work. Thus a life in arts and culture gets harder, even as distribution methods get more efficient.

Open access may make the inequalities in society we have not yet resolved more extreme. There's no app for that. The age of FAANG brings with it challenges that evaluation strategies must learn to deal with. As Julianne Schultz points out:

> we are seeing a massive redistribution of wealth from the
> cultural sector, where meaning is created, to the technology

---

67   Safiya Umoja Noble, *Algorithms of Oppression: How Search Engines Reinforce Racism* (New York: NYU Press, 2018).

sector, which has figured out how to market, distribute, reach and make money out of it in ways the cultural industries never imagined possible.[68]

The role of Google (with its company motto 'Don't be evil' disappearing in 2018[69]) needs particular vigilance. Noble reminds us:

> Digital media platforms like Google and Facebook may disavow responsibility for the results of their algorithms, but they can have tremendous – and disturbing – social effects. Racist and sexist bias, misinformation, and profiling are frequently unnoticed by-products of those algorithms. And unlike public institutions (like the library), Google and Facebook have no transparent curation process by which the public can judge the credibility or legitimacy of the information they propagate.[70]

David Beer calls this 'the social power of algorithms'.[71] If these systems are going to control our experience of culture and our means of communication about it, we have to have better ways of understanding them.

Examined more closely, the notion of digital disruption for arts and culture looks like a sleight of hand. If we leave it to the technology of big data, we will have no meaningful role in curating our stories and creativity. It is hard to see how this would turn out well for a medium-sized Anglophone country with a history of adopting a cargo-cult mentality. For Schultz it's about how we

---

68   Schultz, 'Australia Must Act Now'.
69   Kate Conger, 'Google Removes 'Don't Be Evil' Clause From Its Code Of Conduct' *Gizmodo*. 18 May 2018.
70   Safiya Noble. 'Google and the Misinformed Public', *Chronicle of Higher Education*, 15 January 2017.
71   David Beer, 'The Social Power of Algorithms', *Information, Communication & Society*, 20.1 (2017), 1–13.

value culture in an environment where the currency is 'likes' or 'shares' rather than any kind of deeper engagement:

> The purpose of cultural investment in the Age of FANG
> needs to be restated, funding maintained and opportunities
> to innovate and export enhanced. Otherwise we will become
> invisible at best and tribal at worst. If that happens we will
> be reduced as citizens and countries to passive consumers in
> a digital marketplace that values us only for our ability
> to pay. [72]

---

72 Schultz, 'Australia Must Act Now'.

Box 5 The My Cultural Organisation Website

In 2014, Laboratory Adelaide gave a presentation on our research to the Australian Major Performing Arts Group. We talked about the problems arts and culture face in respect of language, time, and the balancing of quantitative and qualitative information. The usual. We used this thought experiment to illustrate the suffocating hold quantitative data has over our idea of value.

'Some of you', we said, 'will have children in primary or secondary school. So you know all about the MySchool website and how it exists to make transparent 10,000-plus schools in Australia. The site provides "statistical and contextual information" to help parents make good decisions, meaningful decisions, about where to send their children to school. It creates standard entries for each school so that data is comparable across sites. You can see the enrolment numbers, the diversity statistics and the "Index of Community Socio-Educational Advantage" (ICSEA – providing the school's ICSEA value, the Average ICSEA value, and the distribution of students across the index) of the environment in which the school is located.

'School performance is based on the National Assessment Program – Literacy and Numeracy (NAPLAN) tests that students do in years 3,

5, 7 and 9. It tells you how many students are enrolled in each year level. It presents data going back to 2008. It delineates whether the school is government or private, what years it caters for, whether it is metropolitan, rural or remote. How many teaching staff there are and the full-time equivalency (FTE) of those staff. How many non-teaching staff the school employs. Details about a school's finances. The site allows schools to add a context statement so they can tell a narrative about their school and the community in which it is embedded.

'But does anyone really read that? Educators criticise the MySchool site for many reasons. It bases the value of a school on results of a standardised literacy and numeracy test. Teachers say a student's success on the test depends more on whether they got a good sleep the night before or had breakfast than on the quality of teaching they have received.

'What if', we jokingly suggested, 'the quantitative data that arts and cultural organisations are required to collect were used to generate a MyCulturalOrganisation website that the government and the public used to make (supposedly) informed decisions about which cultural activities to invest time and money in?'

To say it again: there is a mismatch between our drive for quantitative data and the quality of information it provides. These are approaches open to significant political pressure, misuse and caricature. They are expensive exercises that divert resources away from meaningful to meaningless evaluation.

CHAPTER FOUR

Parable of Value 3:
The Adelaide Festival of Ideas

This is a chapter about public value, a concept not to be confused with value-for-money. Douglas Muecke once wrote, 'getting to grips with irony [has] something in common with gathering the mist; there is plenty to take hold of, if only one could'.[73] Public value is similarly evident and evasive, real and intangible. In line with the overall thrust of this book, we discuss it here as something that can be contextually assessed but not objectively measured. Guiding questions are more use than a numerical methodology. Who is (or are) the public(s)? What do they value? And what sort of pressure does the concept of public value come under in the modern neoliberal economic order and its demented twin, an insurgent political populism?

If you take Wikipedia's word for it, public value is a recent concept. Coined by Mark H. Moore, Hauser Professor for Nonprofit Organizations at Harvard University, it was seen as the equivalent of shareholder value for public management.[74] This is an interesting illustration of the current obsession with the novelty of buzz-words, because the idea, if not its precise use in policy discourse, goes back much further than the 1990s. It has been a live issue in republican thinking since Periclean Athens, and predates the invention of the

---

73   D.C. Muecke, *The Compass of Irony* (London: Methuen, 1969), 3.
74   Wikipedia, 'Public Value': en.wikipedia.org/wiki/Public_value.

public corporation by some centuries. Its reappearance as a new idea is, to put a positive spin on it, a sign of pushback against the current economic model that frames every human activity as a form of private market exchange. This model has delivered all the benefit it has to bestow. Arguments about public value are a way of picking up the pieces, even if they suffer from amnesia about intellectual history.

Public activities often seek public money. Any time this is spent somewhere, it might arguably have been better spent somewhere else. This is how the South Australian Government attempted to resolve these issues in 2017:

> Public value is an approach to public sector management that puts citizens at the centre of policy, service design and delivery. It … is built around a strategic triangle, comprising three essential areas of consideration when developing and delivering policy and services. Public value is created when the three elements of the strategic triangle are aligned:
>
> 1. Public value – what is the outcome and who is it for?
>
> 2. Legitimacy and support – who do you need to engage to build a satisfactory authorising environment.
>
> 3. Operational capability – how will the outcomes be delivered? What is the cost and what resources are required?[75]

This is fairly representative of current government views in Australia and is an adequate set of principles as long as 'alignment'

---

75 South Australian Department of Premier and Cabinet, *Public Value: Putting Citizens at the Centre of Policy, Service Design and Delivery*, 3: dpc.sa.gov.au/__ data/assets/pdf_file/0019/16660/Public_value_policy_resouce_web.pdf.

is recognised as a matter of judgment and not a technocratic fit. It invites discussion (which is good) and is consequently hard to 'operationalise' in a mechanical manner (which would be bad). Over the last 30 years, attempts to map public value have occurred largely through economic impact studies that aspire to put a dollar value on an opera or a car race. These wore out their welcome with Treasuries around the land. They were projections (which is to say fictions) that could only be assessed for their effects after the money was spent. Those effects were hard to separate from other economic 'noise', while the promise of generating new money for the economy was hard to separate from money that would have been spent on something else anyway. In 2008, the Formula 1 Grand Prix went abruptly from making a profit for Victoria to making a substantial loss because of a change in assessment methods. Economic impact studies could no longer hide the fact that public funding for the race was a political choice. The race is not economically rational – and yet it goes on. For economics is only ever part of the value story.

For Laboratory Adelaide, this is not a scandal, just a recognition of the reality. We have explored an economic contingency evaluation method that asks 'users' and 'non-users' of the Adelaide Festival what they are willing to pay for it from their taxes. We have sent interviewers to Festival events and to suburban shopping centres to ask the same set of questions. Unsurprisingly, the event-goers put a high dollar value on the Festival. Given the Festival's centrality to Adelaide's sense of identity, it was not much more surprising that the non-user dollar figure, though lower, was still very positive. Both sets of numbers were gratifying to our industry partners. Also unsurprisingly the State Treasury did not change their allocation for the Festival to the higher figure we had estimated. We came up with numbers that could be validly used in arguments about the Festival's budget, but not ones that compelled consent.

A dollar value is only ever a partial measure of public value. Art and ideas also create value in themselves, so how can we talk about *that* in a serious way? Let us to turn to our third parable of value: the oldest ideas festival in Australia, the Adelaide Festival of Ideas (AFOI). As a format it was new in 1999, something hard to believe two decades later, now the air is thick with 'thought leaders' flying to one thinkathon or another. In 2001, author Robert Phiddian, associated with the AFOI since its inception, described the first event thus:

> It was a dark and stormy night ... Well, it was dark, and it had been raining all day, and it did look pretty bleak outside. It was Thursday 8th of July 1999, when guests, organisers, and the usual suspects gathered to launch the first Adelaide Festival of Ideas ... In less than a year, we had put together an interesting programme of thinkers from physics to sociology, from politics to theology. Miraculously, everyone who accepted an invitation had arrived. Now all we had to worry about was whether those on an open invitation, the intelligent public of Adelaide, would show up ... Gerard Henderson ... grizzled veteran of the Sydney Institute and many other public lectures, forums, round tables, etc. was heard to express doubt about whether anyone would turn up ... His experience in Sydney was that 30 or 40 constituted a crowd for an intellectual discussion... The next morning dawned bright and fair. We wandered towards the first session in Bonython Hall, but with quickening step as we realised we were in a growing crowd that seemed to have the same goal. By the time we got there – ten minutes before the hour – we had to sit half way up the hall ... The numbers built over the weekend ... The intelligent public of Adelaide – the one that has always supported the Festival, Writers' Week, and the city's proud history of civic debate

and experiment – had found another opportunity to get together to think, listen, and talk.[76]

Who were these people? Where did they come from? What did they want? What were they willing to give? How had they found the event? What did they value about it?

Publics and Benefits

The AFOI is not a profit-driven event. This is often the case in culture, and a central reason why it should never be regarded as simply another industry. The principal funders of cultural activity in Australia are not governments, corporations or philanthropists. First come the artists, then the volunteers and supporters, finally the benefactors. The gift economy, where art and ideas circulate *gratis*, dwarfs the money economy where culture turns a buck. This is not in itself an argument for increased public funding. But it is an assertion that there is a public benefit that occurs in, and through, activities that exceeds the way those activities are publically supported. Value in culture is less monetisable than in spheres such as banking or even healthcare.

For the AFOI, indirect funders include all its comparatively poorly-paid professional staff, from executive producers to event managers, and its large volunteer labour force, from the program advisory committee to helpers on the doors. The main source of capital is goodwill. People involved in the AFOI believe they are doing 'a good thing' for Adelaide, not running a business. The event's purpose is understood as the development of public understanding rather than the dissemination of 'new knowledge' or the provision of 'mere entertainment'. Value is delivered over time, as the growth of a civic culture of insight, one with a history as well as a present and a future. The element of *time* is poorly recognised in policy debates

---

76   Robert Phiddian, 'Parklands of the Mind', *Adelaide Review*, June 2001.

about public value, focused as they are on econometric definitions of return.[77] The living past of the AFOI reflects Adelaide's traditional profile as 'a paradise of dissent' that goes back to the European foundation of the city in the 1830s and 1840s. South Australia was set up as the only 'free' (i.e. free of transported British convicts) Australian colony, and was particularly open to Protestant groups from Britain and Germany. It had a library before it had a settlement in the famous 'trunk of books' that was sent out with the first white settlers.[78] While this colonial heritage is a mixed blessing, one advantage is the expectation born of the Protestant exegetical tradition that public debate is both a right and a duty. The AFOI would have played out differently in other places, as the story of the Chicago Humanities Festival (established 1990) and of the comparatively short-lived Sydney Festival of Dangerous Ideas (2009–16) show.

At the outset, the AFOI's funding came from the state government (initially with few strings attached), supplemented by universities, public interest bodies, and individuals. It has always maintained that the bulk of sessions have to be free so people come as citizens rather than consumers. This cost structure means that it cannot attract the star speakers who command substantial speakers' fees. But it encourages the management to 'future talent-pick', which is arguably more important (and fun). Free access allows people to be promiscuous in their choices, and adventurous in ranging across subject matters. They may have travelled in for a 'last chance to

---

77 See Eleonora Belfiore, '"Impact", "Value" and "Bad Economics": Making Sense of the Problem of Value in the Arts and Humanities', *Arts and Humanities in Higher Education*, 14.1 (2015), 95–110: doi.org/10.1177/1474022214531503; Eleonora Belfiore and Anna Upchurch, *Humanities in the Twenty-First Century: Beyond Utility and Markets* (Basingstoke: Palgrave Macmillan, 2013).

78 Carl Bridge, *A Trunk Full of Books: History of the State Library of South Australia and Its Forerunners* (Adelaide: Wakefield Press in association with the State Library of South Australia, 1986).

hear' a grand old figure like the ecologist James Lovelock, or for the brand recognition of national media personalities like Annabel Crabb and Phillip Adams. But they stay for an eloquent academic or entrepreneur they haven't heard of. It is this sort of communal associative behaviour that contributes so substantially to informed public debate. These benefits are not easily separated from those provided by other, related, cultural events, and they cannot be reduced to a counting of bed-nights and increased restaurant turnover. In a fractious world riven by ugly populisms, the benefits of such social cohesion are, nevertheless, very real.

A few numbers do help communicate the nature of the event. In 2013, the AFOI was attended by 16,000 individuals, amounting to 36,000 attendances at separate sessions across three days, with one-to-four venues operating at any one time. In a city of a million people, this is not as popular as the football, but it is a substantial result for a government outlay of only $250,000. It is fair to say that the AFOI attracts mostly middle-class, older, educated attendees; it is enthusiastic about diversity, but does not appeal to people from all walks of life, as no event does. The politics of its publics are broadly progressive, with a sprinkling of social activists among what author Judith Brett has dubbed 'the moral middle class'. [79] The speakers, too, engage as citizens rather than service providers, often declining a fee or coming for modest remuneration.

Institutional history is a crucial part of this value story. The AFOI started under the auspices of the long-established Adelaide Festival of Arts, and as a sister event to the-then biennial Writers' Week literary festival. For 14 years (eight festivals) its core funding came from the state government. This did not grow with inflation, but allowed the event to remain committed to its original mission

---

79   Judith Brett, *The Australian Liberals and the Moral Middle Class: From Alfred Deakin to John Howard* (Port Melbourne, Vic: Cambridge University Press, 2003).

and aims. There are few company headquarters in Adelaide and thus limited avenues for corporate support, so private sponsorship has enhanced rather than transformed the event. Since 2010 the Festival has been administratively peripatetic, first attached to the Department of Premier and Cabinet (good resources, highly bureaucratic), next to the Film Festival (which helped put on a fine Festival in 2013 then failed to protect its funding). Loss of government support meant that the AFOI missed a year in 2015, then came back in 2016 as an independent event. It presented in 2018 again as an independent event. Why bother? Who benefits from such a hard-fought scramble for resources to put on three days of talk every two years? Yet while living without a dominant funder makes life complicated, it is in several ways a better exist-ence. Corporations and government alike are becoming obsessive about controlling any message they are a party to supporting. Consequently, freedom of discussion is a rare and valuable thing.

The AFOI builds public value in a way that demands careful analysis. Indeed, calling it public value as if it is a sort of commodity can be a distraction. Even for the Festival's fairly homogenous audience, it is better to talk of publics with different experiences of values rather than a single public with just one. There is no more than accidental overlap between the audience attracted by a cosmologist like Paul Davies and one by a controversialist like Naomi Klein or Malaysian leader Anwar Ibrahim. In his seminal book *Publics and Counterpublics*, Michael Warner proposes that publics are 'hailed into being by discourse'[80] – in other words, by communities of interest in particular topics and modes of conversation. These are not social classes or clubs, which people belong to by birth or formal affiliation. They exist only by dint of attendance at events of common interest. The element of voluntary intellectual association

---

80   Michael Warner, *Publics and Counterpublics* (New York: Zone, 2002).

is crucial to the health of liberal democracies.[81] That looks a grand claim for such a small urban event, but similar gatherings attract the authorities' attention (and ire) in Teheran, Beijing, Moscow and Ankara. A crucial part of the value produced occurs in the engagement *around* the event and its ideas. Those who attend the AFOI form loose coalitions whose basis is not commercial or focused on the consumption of a service. The Festival cannot be reduced to a market exchange between a producer and a paying customer. An 'Explainer' about public value put out by the Australia and New Zealand School of Government (ANZSOG) shows how hard it is for those in government to fully comprehend this creative role of publics:

> Like many academic concepts, the meaning of public value is contested – but we think the main difference is really about how the value is consumed. Private value [is] consumed individually ... Public value [is] consumed collectively.[82]

The AFOI may consume small sums of money, but it doesn't 'consume' public value – it builds it. The value of the event is co-created by attendees, and lives on in memories and social formations. A mark of this co-creation is the way that publics have unfailingly found the AFOI even when its marketing has been late or minimal. The scale of attendance is influenced more by the weather than the size of the budget, and the event has always 'worked'. Can you determine whether this 'working' represents a return on investment for funders and those who have contributed

---

81   This reworks material pursued at much greater length in Robert Phiddian, 'The Publics of the Adelaide Festival of Ideas', *University of Toronto Quarterly*, 85.4 (2016), 93–108.

82   ANZOG, 'Public Admin Explainer: What is Public Value?', 10 April 2017: www.anzsog.edu.au/resource-library/research/what-is-public-value.

their labour at 'below market rate'? On the surface, this question is amenable to algorithmic computation. In practice, it is a matter for judgment. The money and effort spent biennially on the AFOI could have been spent on 'saving jobs' or 'funding cancer research'. But in terms of getting an informed and engaged citizenry, it's a defensible expenditure. There is a level of justification no metric can reliably relay because different *sorts* of value, though they need to be politically comparable, cannot be made methodologically commensurable. The point of choice, of value judgment, cannot be measured away, and we would be better off avoiding the false consciousness involved in that quest.

'The Marketplace of Ideas': Beware the Hand of the Dead (Metaphor)!

The AFOI got in early to a boom in public discussion and evangelisation about ideas that washed over the first decades of the twenty-first century like a mud tide. If there has not been a proportional rise in wisdom across the Western world – and who could claim there has? – part of the reason lies in the extent to which the circulation of public value has been subordinated to the language and logic of the market. In an otherwise perceptive book on foreign policy making, David Drezner uses the phrase 'marketplace of ideas' nearly 200 times.[83] In New York, at the centre of US media, the fact that he does so without irony is forgivable – but not accurate. In the realm of metaphors, it is the 'dead' ones that do most ideological damage. The 'marketplace of ideas' is an expression that slides under the horizon of critical consciousness.

---

83 Daniel Drezner, *The Ideas Industry: How Pessimists, Partisans, and Plutocrats Are Transforming the Marketplace of Ideas* (Oxford, New York: Oxford University Press, 2017). A search of the Kindle edition provides 199 matches for 'marketplace' of which only five are for usages other than 'marketplace of ideas' or 'marketplace for foreign policy ideas'.

It's like the constant patter about creative *industries*, a pervasive and partial metaphor for arts and culture in policy discourse. The metaphors become habituated ways of thinking, ones that silently order the world, but bring with them hidden costs.

It should be remembered that ideas do *not* literally engage in a Darwinian struggle for survival that automatically achieves equilibrium.[84] There is a marketplace for *books*, but ideas themselves circulate immaterially. The value they provide is only partly private, and they do not have the characteristics of real property. Consequently, they do not reliably act either like commodities, services or capital. Neither individuals nor corporations can own them. A closer metaphor for their circulation might be 'ecologies', a term that is often now deployed for arts and culture. When things are going well, they endow a public sphere of polite and rational deliberation. Stefan Collini has eloquently described how the marketplace as all-purpose policy trope is killing British higher education policy.[85] Naomi Goulder has aptly summarised his message as 'recognis[ing] the value of cooperative enquiry and creativity – and a H[igher] E[ducation] system in which these values remain enshrined'.[86] Collini's knockdown argument against the remaking of the university sector as a set of market relationships goes like this: were you, in 1980, looking at the relative reputations of British universities and British business, would you draw the conclusion that the former should spend the next few decades remaking itself in the image of the latter? Universities still vestigially remain communities of scholars striving for knowledge

---

84 David Sessions 'The Rise of the Thought Leader', *The New Republic*, 28 June 2017, makes this important critique of the market metaphor in his otherwise admiring piece on Drezner's book.

85 Stefan Collini, *Speaking of Universities* (London and New York: Verso, 2017).

86 Naomi Goulder, 'Books in Brief: Speaking of Universities by Stefan Collini': www.prospectmagazine.co.uk/magazine/books-in-brief-speaking-of-universities-by-stefan-collini.

and wisdom, not bunches of consumers seeking top return for their education dollar. These values apply likewise to the public discussion of ideas. For those involved in making the AFOI 'work', the value of cooperative enquiry captures their communal sense of purpose better than a competitive desire to increase turnover and be the dominant ideas event in the southern hemisphere.

This puts the AFOI very much on one side of a binary distinction Drezner draws between public intellectuals and thought leaders. His main proposition is that these are the two types of 'producers' populating the marketplace of ideas. The former are traditional writers and scholars, holding forth on a range of issues in a way that highlights their complexities and consequences. Their main role is critique, and they often leave issues more intractable than when they picked them up. The latter are thinkers with a Big Idea to sell, a single solution to a Big Problem. Their main roles are prophesy and evangelism, so they are comfortable with the status of celebrity that modern media platforms have extended to them. They spruik patented ideas like 'creative cities' or 'digital disruption' – lots of sudden and clearly mapped change. Drezner points out that circumstances today favour thought leaders over public intellectuals. For the AFOI, the quickest path to exposure and money would be to program a raft of futurists. There is always an appetite for vivid predictions, one unslaked by persistent disappointment. Given its commitment to informed civic discussion, however, the AFOI cannot do this with a clear conscience.

A reductive economic view would see speakers at ideas events as trader-entertainers. Certainly, successful public talkers are entertain*ing*, with public intellectuals tending to wry humour or charismatic gloom, and thought leaders to sermonic fervour. There is theatre and rhetoric in public ideas, not just sober propositional content. The trouble is that cogent critical opinion is seldom designed for easy consumption or frictionless results. Those making the case for the difficult retrenchments necessary to address climate change, for example, do not offer instant answers, so run the risk of being drowned out by glib techno-utopian solutions or reactionary denial. It is a fair criticism to say that public intellectuals are prone to 'virtue signalling'. They provide few easy solutions to difficult problems, in contrast to the thought leaders, who provide too many. This can be exhilarating for audiences, but sometimes dangerous for public value. Michael Sessions points to the risk for public intellectuals of entanglement in the postmodern patronage system, dubbed philanthrocapitalism.[87] This involves selling something in the marketplace of ideas (thus accepting the metaphor) and appealing to rich and powerful patrons to make that vision a reality. This is not a new strategy. Voltaire's commitment to robust debate was briefly muffled by his sojourn at the court of Frederick the Great in the 1750s. But it is increasingly pervasive today, as the rich become super-rich and seek vindication, apologia or redemption for growing global inequality. Individual philanthropists who have made their fortunes in recent decades show great faith in technological innovation particularly, often the basis of their own financial success. They prefer technical solutions to complex issues over democratic discussion about them. They trust that the market can be left to deliver equity (if you carry a hammer, every problem looks like a nail). Thought leaders seized of the importance of their missions shape their ideas to the pockets of their potential sponsors.

The obvious contrast to a socially associative event like the AFOI is the 'ideas business' of TEDx. TEDx started as a commercial concern, charging for entry, and it has always tended to glossy entrepreneurial packages rather than earnest worrying at perennial questions. Charismatic 20-minute monologues on resolving the

---

87   Sessions (2017); the word is not his and has been around for at least a decade ('The Birth of Philanthrocapitalism', *The Economist*, 23 February 2006).

world's disorders are the perfect product for the marketplace of ideas. But in the end, it is the oversimplification of TEDx talks – their commitment to glib solution and their dissolution of complication – that should give us pause. Too many of them are exercises in banal futurism, the sort of cunning prophesy that makes no real contribution to human understanding, though the most successful ones (those over 10 million watches, if you sort TEDx talks by popularity) are predominantly inspirational talks about leadership. This promise of instant results cannot begin to grapple with difficult issues. Rich and layered dialogue, not jejune formulations, is the only way, for example, to achieve reconciliation between Aboriginal peoples and Australia's successive waves of immigrant settlers. Intellectual leadership requires the patience to resist easy solutions, even in the face of urgent need. This shows up the trouble with thought leaders: they too often overreach when their Big Idea is taken beyond its orbit of relevance.

For two decades the AFOI has been building public value without having anything particularly shiny to sell. It has resisted philanthrocapitalism, or chased it only half-heartedly. Public value, open dialogue, good causes, and public intellectuals; these are its loyalties. Its main genres have been the lecture, the interview and the panel; discussions more than solutions; complexity and wonder more than simplicity and technical fix. The AFOI strongly suggests that marketplace-like competition is a poor way to understand how ideas and culture best flourish. It reduces a wide range of phenomena to a small number of causal factors. It assumes that any successful event must want to grow endlessly. Yet the current business plan of the Festival does not scale up. It has a civic 'bite' that belongs in a particular place with natural limitations. The experience of the AFOI cannot be abstracted and decanted into an index or an international speaking franchise. The journey of this medium-sized festival tells a parable of value for a specific public. It is not a dollar value, but it is value nonetheless. Over time, that value grows but perhaps scandalously the AFOI has no ambition to grow as an event. Those running it already think it 'fit for purpose'.

Since the Global Financial Crisis of 2007–08, there has been growing questioning of market models of value both from within economics and without. Meanwhile, beware the undead metaphor, the pervasive zombie metaphor of the market. At the moment it may feel like the only way of conceiving of culture's value is via more 'agility' in pursuit of 'customer opportunity'. But, as John Quiggin and many others argue, the neoclassical economics of Pareto-optimal efficiency is in collapse.[88] So much of what is valuable in the circulation of ideas is intangible, cooperative and creative. The benefits look more like a gift than a transaction.

Public value is the result of mindful persuasion. It can be evidenced, experienced and witnessed, discussed and disputed. In a world with limited resources – the only sort of world we will ever have – different instances of value have to be ranked when it comes to handing out public money. But the ranking will always be a political choice, in the richest and best sense of that phrase. It will be a judgment with social consequences, and as such open to revision. In one generation, it seems good to put up a statue to Captain Cook or Lachlan Macquarie; in another it seems good to take them down. These *revaluations* can be understood historically and descriptively, but to ascribe them to a rise and fall in a marketplace of value is a tautology produced by ideological idiocy.

---

88   For entry points to a rich literature, see Thomas Piketty and Arthur Goldhammer, *Capital in the Twenty-First Century* (Cambridge Massachusetts: The Belknap Press of Harvard University Press, 2014); John Quiggin, *Zombie Economics: How Dead Ideas Still Walk among Us* (Princeton: Princeton University Press, 2010); Richard M. Bookstaber, *The End of Theory: Financial Crises, the Failure of Economics, and the Sweep of Human Interaction* (Princeton: Princeton University Press, 2017); John Lanchester, *Whoops! Why Everyone Owes Everyone and No One Can Pay* (London: Penguin, 2010).

Box 6 Long-term Value: The South Australian Red Cross Information Bureau and the State Library of South Australia, by Heather Robinson

The State Library of South Australia [SLSA] is the keeper of the state's official public memory. This is an inescapably political role that often courts conflict among differing perceptions of value. Public memories are made from documents and artefacts collected over time, preserved in perpetuity and activated when curiosity or a need arises. Their value is then realised, sometimes decades after an item's collection. Their use and engagement may have been unknowable for much of their existence. They may have laid forgotten in the stacks, their place obscured by inaccessibility, changing tastes, or political priorities. Only the most vigilant archivists may have seen them, awaiting the confluence of time, interest and in some cases, technology, for their value to become apparent.

The records of the South Australian Red Cross Information Bureau (SARCIB) were donated to the library in 1919, as evidence of the fate of South Australian soldiers serving in World War I. A file was opened each time a family member enquired about a missing soldier. They may not have heard from them or the war department for months, or had received heartbreakingly ambiguous or truncated statements regarding their state of health or deaths. To address such queries, the Red Cross established information bureaux in most Australian capital cities, coordinating through a central office in Melbourne with British and European offices. Staffed by volunteers, the bureau in Adelaide was located in the newly constructed Verco Buildings, diagonally opposite the State Library of South Australia. Throughout the war, the library continued to operate with a staff reduced by conscription, budget cuts and casualties. Members of staff and the Board raised funds, and promoted patriotic books, maps and publications on the countries at war.

Sir Josiah Symon KC, one of the library's prominent benefactors and a leading lawyer, was appointed Chair of the SARCIB General

Committee. Symon had been influential in persuading members of the legal profession to 'enlist' as Volunteer Searchers for bureaux around the country, as 'their trained minds and experience in investigation will be of great advantage in investigating and dealing with the enquiries'. This 'small core group' worked alongside clerical volunteers who would compile dossiers for every enquiry, noting each step taken and any details gathered in the search. Once cross-checked with other available documentation, new information would be forwarded to the enquirer.

Between December 1915 and the end of the war, SARCIB compiled 8,000 files responding to enquiries by members of the public. In 1920, when the bureau closed its doors, Symon instigated the final transfer of the collection to the State Library of South Australia. No other Australian bureau kept their files. Perhaps Symon, in his patriotic fervor, recognised how the dossiers encapsulated the experience of the soldiers, the camaraderie between those who witnessed their passing and the prolonged anguish of the families. Collectively, the packets were a record of South Australia's experience of that war, kept in the belief that one day they might be required as a window on a community in a time of crisis.

In 2012, a conversation between Andrew Piper, a SLSA project leader, and an interstate colleague turned to their respective institutions' plans to commemorate the centenary of World War I. Piper recalled a box full of Red Cross files that were searchable only through antiquated microfiche. Over the years, archivists had attempted to interpret the complex series of regimental numbers and codes. However, with little demand since the war's end, they lacked an institutional priority to do more than preserve and protect them. Calling in favours from staff and a team of volunteers, Piper steered a three-year digitisation project, creating a database and website that made publically available the documents of official correspondence about soldiers' whereabouts or their final moments.

The South Australian Red Cross Information Bureau website was launched with an exhibition by the SLSA in February 2016, linking the SARCIB information with related documents at the National Archives of Australia, the War Memorial and TROVE via technologies unimaginable at the time the documents were first compiled. The resource filled critical gaps for surviving family members. On viewing the documents for the first time, Mr Winter spoke of his grandfather, who never shared his experience of the war with his family:

> It's great future generations of my family, and others, get a sense of what these guys did and what was happening back home … I knew he was in it but that was it.

In August 2016, the State Theatre Company of South Australia presented *Red Cross Letters*, a live performance based on stories drawn from selected SARCIB packets. The production toured South Australian regional and urban centres and included sessions featuring SLSA representatives speaking about their role in reactivating the documents.

In 2017, in recognition of this project, the SLSA was awarded a Red Cross Humanitarian Partner Award. This online portal to the collection is accessible worldwide, a testament to South Australia's experience of war for generations to come. It attracts around 1,000 visitors per month.

'What I never knew about my war hero grandfather: State Library's South Australia Red Cross Information Bureau Collection', *Adelaide Now,* 22 February, 2016; see https://sarcib.ww1.collections.slsa.sa.gov.au/.

Part II

WHERE TO FROM HERE?

CHAPTER FIVE

The Language of Value

'I know all those words, but that sentence
makes no sense to me.'
Matt Groening, writer of *The Simpsons*

On the Importance of Not Being an Expert

Language matters. It is our most important tool for thinking and living together. Consider a common scenario. A problem of public importance is raised – in the media, parliament, or by citizens' petition. The problem might be concrete and directly observable: for example, a lack of inner city housing or the length of surgery waiting lists. Or it may be understandable only in a conceptual way: for example, the youth crime rate or the level of inflation. The problem is then defined, discussed and pronounced upon by experts. Experts vary as much as the problems they address. Some experts draw on practical experience to assert their status. Others are credited through academic or clinical study. Called from their life of expertise into the public eye, they then interpret some aspect of the common world. There is no physical 'look' that signals an expert – though middle-aged, white men are well represented. They may dress in a suit and tie or a T-shirt that looks like it's been used to mop up spilt gravy. What they share, however, is 'expert talk'. Expert talk is a type of communication that aspires to leave hearers in no doubt they are getting important information, whether or not they understand it themselves. Think of the dialogue in a TV hospital soap opera. What do the doctors mean when they say that a patient has 'a high-grade fixed artery stenosis caused by atherosclerosis and coronary vasospasm'. We have no idea. Well, actually we have *one* idea: that they know what they are talking about. And because of this, we defer to them. Their view is more than mere opinion (the ancient Greek word is *doxa)*. It is a *judgment* (the ancient Greek word is *krisis)*.

The basis of all expert talk is informed comparison. Whether it takes the form of legal opinion, medical diagnosis, critical review or mathematical algorithm, the foundation on which expertise is built is comparative knowledge. Comparison begets measurement, and measurement enables comparison. Faced with two things, or the same thing on two different occasions, we face a need to relate, equate and benchmark. Sometimes measurement and comparison are so closely intertwined as to be indistinguishable. To seek expert knowledge about health, wealth and level of reading skill is to seek it about their opposites: illness, poverty and illiteracy. Many things exist on a spectrum of contrasting instances. These are organised under collective nouns – statisticians call them 'nominative categories' – and in an almost inevitable sleight of hand, as categories suck in the instances around them like a whirlpool, comparison takes on the authority of broad generalisation: the authority of experts is connected to their use of language.

Yet here a doubt rings out like a ship's bell. How convincing are these generalisations and what exactly does expert talk prove? Does it inform consent or merely demand it? When should we accede to experts, and when should we demur? In an age of self-seeking elites and caustic populists, these are not abstract questions. What does it mean to be told that we are 'objectively obese', 'a below-average wage earner' or 'a typical school leaver'? In passing from instance to category, the single phenomenon to the collective noun, our own personal experience will sometimes stubbornly refuse to pluralise. In fact, the whole edifice of expert explanation hits a wall when it comes to what happens on an individual level. No-one cares about their conformance to a Gaussian bell curve of normal distribution if they do not *feel* fat or poor or a typical anything.

People's states of mind determine certain issues, and while these can be sensibly framed, they cannot be settled by expert fiat. In one pre-Brexit meeting organised by the UK's Remain party, a Treasury spokesperson pointed to the country's rising GDP, whereupon someone from the audience shouted 'that's not *my* GDP'. Here expert talk fails, and the categories used to organise the instances around it are exposed as hollow fictions. The further you go into the personal realm, the more things resist expert generalisation. What is a typical dream? A normal love affair? An average poem? Knowing that there are many metrically similar sonnet lines to 'Shall I compare thee to a summer's day?' tells you something. But not a lot.

Expert talk is limited in these areas because it abuts onto a mysterious continent we might call, for the sake of brevity, 'being human'. Here, being healthy, wealthy and wise is a matter for inner adjudication rather than external calibration. Some judgments we have to make for ourselves. No-one can tell us we are happy if we don't feel it, or offer more than generic advice when it comes to the direction of our own lives. We can listen to the views of others, but cannot outsource our problems to them. The recalcitrance of individual experience is especially relevant to the evaluation of culture. The building of bridges may be a matter of dispassionate knowledge, as they need to stand up more than they need to be aesthetically pleasing. But cultural experience is 'always already' personal. You might go to the theatre often, but each occasion is different. Even re-reading a book or re-watching a film are new events compared to first exposure. Moreover, because culture is both all around us, defining our way of life, and a discrete set of arts practices, it prompts our widest responses. Some aspects of culture can be compared, measured and generalised. Others can't, and the challenge is to evaluate them by carefully discerning their place in our own hearts and minds. Expert talk has a role to play, as guide or provocateur. We can read reviews and blog posts with profit and pleasure. But the arguments they marshal are always extruded through someone's personal understanding. As in our democratic political realm, where each citizen has a right to one vote, the cultural realm is predicated on a presumed equality of individual response. These many, notionally equal points of judgment are where the evaluation of culture occurs. If we think someone's opinion of a bit of art is wrong, we can't take them to the High Court. Many people hold Shakespeare to be a great writer. But if someone disagrees, we can't point to a bar chart of statistical proof. We have to tackle their view head-on, talking it through and trying to change their mind.

All this highlights the centrality of language to the evaluation of culture. There are a number of types of expert talk that make an appearance here and, like the dialogue in a medical soap, we may recognise their tone even when we don't know exactly what they're saying. The oldest is 'high culture talk', where venerated critics deliver their verdicts on Matthew Arnold's 'best that has been thought and said in the world'. The newest is 'creative industries talk' and its spin-offs 'creative cities talk' and 'creative classes talk'. These mix analysis of cultural practices with discussion about urban regeneration and economic development. In Western countries where a substantial part of the manufacturing base has been lost, culture is often put forward as a solution to post-industrial reinvention, with the arts linked to emerging businesses in advertising or software design. A third type of talk is the functional vocabulary of government policy, seemingly designed to leach out the human qualities of cultural activities by sweeping them into categories so bland as to lack descriptive force entirely. The federal government's Budget papers, for example, refer to 'the cultural function' and 'the cultural subfunctions'. For anyone not inducted into the policy club, what these dispiriting catch-alls include is impossible to guess.

Each kind of expert talk about culture is useful in one context or another, and tells us something about how to approach our own evaluations. What they do not do, however, *cannot* do, is do our thinking for us. However erudite an expert might be – and some are deeply knowledgeable and perceptive – they cannot claim that their *experience* of culture is better than ours. Command of objective data is no substitute for depth of personal response. Our separate cultural experiences mean we will arrive at separate judgments about them. These judgments will be shareable and defensible only if our common language allows for wide-ranging and deep-rooted discussion. Where talk about culture is both informed and aware of culture's true nature, discussion will achieve a proper scope, intensity and register. It will be a dialogue that accumulates insights over time. But these insights will not aggregate nor be eternal.

How to achieve this desirable outcome? The aim here, it is important to remember, is not to *agree* about culture, but to get better at *disagreeing* about it. All participants, professionals and 'mere' citizens must learn to talk better as enthusiastic and well-informed amateurs: as *non-experts*. To bridge the personal and the political, culture talk needs a robust pluralism of positions and tones. This requires language skills as arduously acquired and profound as any expert talk.

Buzzword Bingo

'The whole party were assembled, excepting Frank Churchill,
who was expected every moment from Richmond; and
Mrs. Elton, in all her apparatus of happiness, her large
bonnet and her basket, was very ready to lead the way …
strawberries, and only strawberries,
could now be thought or spoken of.'
Jane Austen, *Emma*

The chicken was memorably inedible; rubbery and insipidly seasoned. The quality of the talk was not much better. This is no criticism of the veterans of the Adelaide arts community, roped-in to a Council for Economic Development (CEDA) lunch on 'Innovation and the Arts' in April 2016. They were doing their best with wearisome material. Cornered by language that had no place for the real purposes of the arts, they were bravely bullshitting to protect their organisations and the cultural sector. They responded as leaders should to a call for public discussion of the term *de jour*. But it was still indigestible. Bad faith, even in a good cause, is hard to hide.

What brought them to this pass? A year earlier George Brandis had turned arts funding on its head by carving away the Australia Council's funding for his NPEA. The sector recalibrated its rhetoric to talk of excellence and only excellence. For all his manifest problems, Brandis was a minister with a genuine passion for the arts. It was obvious why he had thrust excellence into the policy limelight, and what he meant by it. Few people in arts and culture shared his view, but government money is always scarce, and anyone who could play the 'excellence card' with a moderately clear conscience did so. In the 2,719 submissions to the 2015

THE LANGUAGE OF VALUE

Senate Inquiry into the arts cuts, 'excellence' appears 3,406 times, well ahead of 'industry' (2,056), 'access' (1,731), and 'innovation' (a paltry 742). But then Malcolm Turnbull replaced Tony Abbott as Prime Minister and Brandis was relieved of his arts portfolio in a cabinet reshuffle. The bland Mitch Fifield took over a reconfigured Ministry of Communication and the Arts. Peace (a sort of low-level hostile neglect) settled on cultural policy, as Fifield set about anaesthetising the sector and quietly dismantling Brandis's changes. In November, he subsumed the government's arts priorities into those of communications, changing the dominant rhetoric to 'innovation and participation'.[89]

'The last shall be first, and the first last' (Matthew 20.16). Cultural leaders spent their summers clearing 'excellence' from their documents and replacing it with the word 'innovation' in the game of Buzzword Bingo. The lunch of the rubber chickens was the fruit of that work. Now everything from rehanging art galleries thematically to putting orchestra musicians on part-time contracts was dressed as 'innovative'. Rupert Myer, giving the keynote as Chair of the Australia Council, did the big picture alignment with the federal government's agenda, as reported in the next day's Adelaide *Advertiser*:

> The intersection of the arts and innovation was at the heart
> of the products [Steve] Jobs produced and a key to Apple's
> success. The arts embrace broad expressions of human
> creative skill and imagination. And while innovation
> is commonly seen as technology driven, it is present
> in all human endeavour – in science, medicine, social

---

89   Australian Department of Communication and the Arts, 'Catalyst – Australian
     Arts and Culture Fund': www.arts.gov.au/what-we-do/performing-arts/catalyst-
     australian-arts-and-culture-fund.

> development, the environment and the arts. Innovation expands our understanding of the human condition, furthering our insights into cultural systems and values, who we are as a people and a nation.[90]

Such language is not entirely wrong or dishonest. It just doesn't mean much, and the contributions to the CEDA discussion of 'Innovation and the Arts' told us little about creative arts practices or cultural development. Rupert Myer may have been speaking to the sector, but he was not speaking in terms ordinary practitioners or audiences could understand. The collective nouns through which so much policy discussion about arts and culture gets channelled are more of a distraction than an aid. The three most enduring – 'innovation', 'excellence' and 'access' – often seem to cycle through on a mental Lazy Susan. Others, like 'impact', 'sustainability', 'vibrancy' and 'disruption', have seasonal vogues. The difficulty is the misleading belief that a word meaningful in concrete situations (an adjective or specific noun) can generate a general category that transcends concrete instances in a varied field. With our rising faith in big data comes the accompanying assumption that differences in form and context wash out with big numbers. But because of the personal nature of cultural experiences, differences actually *multiply* rather than diminish, with the result that the words of largest scope have the least meaning. 'Innovation' can be attached to nearly anything, and in Fifield's domain it generally was.

Consider the problem in the adjacent space of government-funded university scholarship. Australian universities have been dogged for decades by the search for a quick way of measuring the benefit of their research. Certainly, this has many 'impacts' and any competent government will be concerned to assess these. It does

---

90   Rupert Myer, 'If You Really Want to Lead the World in Innovation, Then Hire an Artist and Let Them Inspire', *The Advertiser*, 29 April 2016, 22.

not follow that every example of good research suggests a general term of evaluation. Even where it does, it may not be measurable. CSIRO scientists invented wi-fi and Monash University medics invented the bionic ear. These had important consequences, but they are not comparable, and it is meaningless to put them on a scale of 1 to 10. Even if such a scale were constructed, it would tell little about where to award the *next* grant. Bionic ear researchers always aimed to help the deaf. CSIRO invented wi-fi as a side-benefit of a failed experiment in particle physics. While it may seem just to reward such luck, there is little rationality in investing in it happening over and over again.

In the language of assessment, loss of meaning can happen at any step, but because it often happens incrementally it may escape attention. An excellent cup of coffee is a real, singular experience. An excellent coffee shop is a place where a lot of excellent cups of coffee are made. Excellence in coffee-making is starting to lose touch with any concrete meaning of excellent, especially if we generalise it across different styles and markets (excellent coffee looks very different in Minneapolis, Melbourne and Medina). By the time we reach 'excellence in food and beverage provision' we are telling ourselves nothing useful about the quality of coffee, or whether a café is open on Sundays. There are further levels of abstraction government language will push, etiolating context even further. But a little of this goes a long way, and a little more leads to the evaporation of meaning entirely.

To be committed to 'excellence' or 'innovation' would be no more than irritating motherhood statements were it not that the policy process deploys such general terms to justify its decisions when resources must be allocated between unlike things. Don Watson has written a number of books criticising this wooden, reductive and alarming use of language. In *Death Sentence* (2003), he invokes the spirit of George Orwell to warn against its numbing effects:

> No doubt in the place from which these words came they
> were judged competent. But they are not competent in the
> world at large. They are not competent as language. They
> represent an example of what Orwell calls anaesthetic
> writing. You cannot read it without losing some level of
> consciousness. You come to, and read it again, and still your
> brain will not reveal the meaning – will not even try. You
> are getting sleepy again.[91]

Watson points out the problem, and we all laugh. But the objects of ridicule refuse to melt away. Children born when *Death Sentence* was first published are now in secondary school. In arts and cultural policy, it would be hard to find anyone who believes language has improved in the last 15 years. Why? It is tempting to see it as a power play by bureaucrats, bending free spirits to their bleak and narrow will. But Watson puts it down to habituation, suggesting that 'corporate leaders have good reasons to twist their language into knots and obscure the meaning of it, but more often it is simply habit'.[92] People write and demand anaesthetic prose less because they are driving towards clear targets than because they are trying to control risk. James Button's brief, unhappy experience in Canberra as a frustrated speechwriter for Kevin Rudd led him to the conclusion that 'the paradox of bad public language' is that 'what looks to outsiders like an exercise of power, an intent to shut others out, in fact expresses a kind of powerlessness'.[93] Anaesthetic prose gestures at getting things done, but its baroque vagueness reflects an anxiety of being caught saying something unambiguous that could prove wrong. If you add the overuse of managerial terms

91   Don Watson, *Death Sentence: The Decay of Public Language* (Milsons Point, NSW: Vintage Australia, 2004), 7.
92   Watson, *Death Sentence*, 35.
93   James Button, *Speechless: A Year in my Father's Business* (Carlton, Vic: Melbourne University Press, 2012), 168.

to basic human fear, you have the ingredients for a tsunami of bullshit.[94]

Of purveyors of anaesthetic language, Watson comments that 'they have forgotten the other way of speaking: the one in which you try to say what you mean'.[95] It is an arresting proposition; the way of speaking our state arts leaders called for at the first Laboratory Adelaide lunch. They *should* be able to talk to government about what really matters rather than laundering their talk through nebulous abstract nouns, passive verbs and opaque categories. They *should* be able to stop worrying about elaborate attempts to demonstrate 'strategic' value that descend into bathos, and to focus on meaningful descriptions of how cultural organisations actually work. Anyone can align to the current clutch of collective nouns, and tack to reflect changes in policy priorities when they occur. The undignified rush to 'innovation' at the CEDA lunch showed this clearly.

Meaningful judgments about culture's value cannot be rendered in anaesthetic prose. Anyone can write defensively when they fear criticism (and probably will). Nevertheless, the Safe Zone of Blah should be resisted. Watson is right to insist that this type of expert talk (the worst) drains things of their meaning and resonance. However, we are not about to enter a world where this language disappears entirely. It is handy for persiflage and sometimes functionally useful. So how can we tame its abstractions for arts and culture? Laboratory Adelaide has developed a handy nine-part writing guide:

---

94 For a philosophical perspective, see Harry G. Frankfurt, *On Bullshit* (Princeton, N.J: Princeton University Press, 2005).

95 Watson, *Death Sentence*, 36.

Box 7 A Guide to Writing about Value

1. **Good writing skills are not peripheral to the provision of evidence: they are the key to it.** The first principle in any evaluation strategy is that rhetoric and the use of rhetorical skills are unavoidable, even in the most data-driven or bureaucratic document. Words can be used well or badly, but they are always required to make some sort of case. Evidence for value in culture does not exist independently of the words used to frame and describe that case.

2. **Because writing is part of making a case, it should not be entirely outsourced.** By all means get capable advice on writing and editing. But the bland polish of consultants will not make your case well. Write yourself if possible, or in close connection with a ghost-writer if necessary.

3. **Write to communicate not to obfuscate.** The language you use should be as simple and direct as the evidence will permit, without being reductive.

4. **Be specific.** Avoid abstract nouns as far as possible. Talk of 'excellent paintings' or 'excellent films', not of 'excellence'. Be concrete in all descriptions.

5. **Carefully attend to the story you are telling.** Present clear narratives, both in anecdotes and in the overall framing of documents. (See the next chapter 'Narratives of Value'.)

6. **Keep bullshit to a minimum.** Only engage in bullshit when there is a clear danger in not doing so. It is a dangerous habit to insult the intelligence of your readers. If we talk to others in a distracted tongue, we will soon start talking to ourselves the same way.

7. **Be truthful.** It is better to go down saying what you truly believe than in a flailing manipulation of fashionable clichés. Culture is a field of endless creative potential, so there will never be enough resources to fund everything worthwhile. It is better to win support honestly when it is won at all.

8. **Be credible.** Build trust over time by presenting credible and consistent narratives, ones that speak of an artist's or cultural organisation's core purposes. A bit of 'alignment with priorities' is acceptable, but a sector that develops a reputation for saying anything for money will not prosper in the long run.

9. **Read as carefully as you write.** Reading is important and, though last in this list, should be first in practice. We expect the documents we write to be carefully read by others, so we should give their documents the same attention. The only real training for good writing is extensive reading.

This list sounds like no more than useful health advice (eat well, exercise regularly, get plenty of sleep). Yet in Laboratory Adelaide's view, communicating well about the value of culture is overwhelmingly a matter of clarity and honesty. Successful evaluation strategies require eloquence not just an abacus, and the eloquence that succeeds comes from truth and precise expression. The above points do not provide a boilerplate for how to talk about culture, though. Every time we make an industry presentation, someone asks us if we have a 'new language of value'. There isn't one. There is no expert talk that will demonstrate definitively what nearly everyone knows intuitively: that culture has a personal value that exceeds its general proofs. Arts managers and practitioners can, however, follow some simple language principles for having a better public conversation about it. It is the business of rational persuasion, as old as Aristotle and as new as the impassioned responses to the 2015 arts cuts Senate Inquiry.

CHAPTER SIX

Narratives of Value

Different Kinds of Value

In China Miévelle's 'new weird' cult classic *The City and the City*, two different populations inhabit a single urban space. One town is 'cross-hatched' by dual existential zones, each with their own history, industry, and jurisdictional powers. The way people cope with being a member of one city but not the other is via an elaborate and tightly policed system of disattention. They 'unsee' and 'unhear' things that belong to one metropolis rather than another. They develop selective ways of understanding that come to seem normal. Whatever exists by way of a physical reality 'out there' is invested by a ubiquitous mental force determining citizens' inner sense of it. In the end, what makes a city a city, it seems, is not density of housing but density of meaning.[96]

What Miévelle describes is evaluation *in extremis*. It might seem a bizarre example to choose, until you remember the codes of religion, class, gender and race that have divided real cities as absolutely as his Bezel and Ul Qomo. These render employees invisible to their employers, and define some human beings as property, to be treated with no more consideration than a garden spade. Readers can perhaps also recall moments when they have 'unseen' the homeless in the streets, or 'unheard' an all-too-public row between friends.

---

96   China Miévelle, *The City and the City* (London: Macmillan, 2009).

There is a great deal of selectivity in what gets noticed, and when controversies erupt they are invariably interpreted according to pre-existing beliefs. There is no better illustration of this than the storm in 2016 over Bill Leak's cartoon of an Aboriginal father so far gone in drink as not to remember his son's name.[97] Some people wanted it prosecuted as incitement to racial vilification, while others defended it as shining a light on systemic child abuse. It was hard to find a middle ground. One person's highly offensive cartoon is another's urgent political truth.

The value of Leak's cartoon was contested, and will remain so. Talk of the 'average' reaction is meaningless. An aggregate of responses would indicate little beyond the fact that its message struck a chord. It only begins to have significance when seen through the frames of Australian race relations, or freedom of expression.

Approaching the problem of value in this way opens it up more broadly, conjoining the smallest decisions we make to the most portentous, and further unpicking the econometric fiction of the free and sovereign consumer. Take Christmas, for example, 'the festive season'. In Australia this is nominally a Christian occasion, the celebration of the birth of Christ. It also occurs at the start of the summer holidays, and involves a complex set of choices about family, friends, budgets and recreational pursuits. Whom to see, where, for how long, and what to bring are questions that exercise everybody's mind in a complex collective rite.

Some of the choices people make at Christmas monetise easily and in these instances talk about 'value for money' is reasonable. Should I drink champagne or white wine? Should I eat fruitcake or Pavlova? Others are monetisable, but have non-monetary implications.

---

97   The cartoon was published in *The Australian*, 4 August 2016, and is available in many places on the internet, for example in Leak's official site at www. theaustralian.com.au/opinion/cartoons/bleak-gallery/image-gallery/ ee8a4ef1032a9da5a37c87ecb7f34c5c.

Should I give my child an Xbox or an encyclopedia? Should I give my partner a DVD set or a share in a Third World goat? Or should I not give at all, as a rebuke to the rampant consumerism of what is supposed to be a religious event? Other choices resist reduction to money entirely. Should I spend Christmas Day with relatives or friends? Or alone, and have time for myself? Time is not money, however hard the monopolists of the internet try to fiscalise it. There are 86,400 seconds in a day and it is a temporal limit no-one has yet transcended. To have Christmas with family members in Queensland is not to have it with friends in New South Wales. The choice is between two experiences that cannot be expressed as trade-offs on an economist's indifference curve except in a gross and unilluminating way.

Evaluation takes place on different registers at once. When I shop for Christmas lunch, I consider tastes other than my own. When I choose which blockbuster film to see on Boxing Day, I juggle expectations that range from those of a child to those of a grandparent. These decisions have an economic aspect to them – it's expensive to take 12 people to the movies. But they also have psychological, ethical and religious aspects. As individuals we are not a unified set of market preferences, but human-beings-in-the-round, living life as we find it: now economic, now emotive, now political, etc. The burgeoning field of behavioural economics tries to grapple with just this range of human 'endowment'. Daniel Kahneman writes impishly:

> Professor R ... was a firm believer in standard economic
> theory as well as a sophisticated wine lover. [Yet he] was
> very reluctant to sell a bottle from his collection – even at
> the high price of $100 (in 1975 dollars!). Professor R bought
> wine at auction, but would never pay more than $35 for a
> bottle of that quality. At prices between $35 and $100, he
> would neither buy nor sell. The large gap is inconsistent with

economic theory, in which the Professor [could be] expected to have a single value for the bottle. If a particular bottle is worth $50 to him, then he should be willing to sell it for any amount in excess of $50. If he did not own the bottle, he should be willing to pay any amount up to $50 for it.[98]

The story illustrates the unrealistic way value is conceived in conventional economics. Certain choices may seem irrational, but this is to refuse to see that sometimes people act in accordance with one set of priorities rather than another. What determines our decisions is not their susceptibility to mathematical computation but the fact that they are meaningful to us, even when we are choosing between incommensurable things: between buying a toaster and buying an airline ticket to see a childhood mate; or between known and unknown experiences. Economists could argue the latter is 'risk-based consumption', and so monetisable. But it is more honest, if more challenging, to say that we sometimes *don't know* what we are choosing, and it is precisely *because* of this that we choose it. We want to try something new. Not a 'new' iteration of a known good or service – an iPhone 8 to replace our iPhone 7 – but something entirely different, like going without a mobile phone at all. Such radical not-knowingness has value too. Perhaps an algorithm can be designed to 'map' our choices with predictive power. But that would not explain them.

Whatever form they take, our cultural choices have meaning, and the process of weighing different options must deal with those meanings in their manifold complexity. The meaning can be direct and vivid; or it can be circuitous and hard to express. I might dress well to go to a party, but when I get there not want to talk to anybody. I might choose to see an exhibition because I 'can't not go' rather than because I have an interest in the artwork on display. I might

---

98   Daniel Kahneman, *Thinking, Fast and Slow* (London: Allen Lane, 2011), 292–93.

listen to music because I know somebody who knows somebody who likes it, rather than because I warm to it myself. Or see a show because it has one scene in it that speaks to me while the rest of it is forgettable. If 'value for money' inhabits a Newtonian world of non-contradictory mechanical forces, 'value as meaning' behaves like a subatomic particle, at one moment unplaceable, the next in multiple locations, delivering a complex cognitive charge that anyone who has had to choose between doing the easy thing, the expected thing, and the right thing, knows well.

Taken seriously, evaluation is one of the most demanding activities we engage in. People do not subject their choices to a uniform standard of self-interest or deliberative rigour. They skip between different registers of sense and weight; measuring, certainly, but also guessing, groping and grabbing as they make decisions about value based on different existential grounds. Like the inhabitants in Miévelle's cities 'unseeing' each other, even when the outcomes of our choices materially coincide, their meaning can be divergent. Many people might support a community choir. For some it is an expression of local loyalty; for others an interest in group singing; for others an opportunity to get out and be part of a social gathering; for others, a mix of all three. Quantitative data can be used to find patterns at the level of statistical population, but the act of *choosing* occurs in this subjective, intuitive crucible.

Meaning is key to evaluation, and time is key to meaning. Choices entail consequences that deliver at different moments in people's lives, some in the short term, some in the medium, some in the long. The decision to subscribe to Netflix meets a more-or-less immediate desire. The decision to learn the violin is one whose benefit will take years to accrue. This is not a simple consumer choice, because the time-scales are vastly different. But for creatures who live in time, human beings have such a poor sense of it. Memories of the past (retrospective memory) are divided into three components:

procedural, semantic and episodic, of which the last is the most important, since it is where people store their most personal recollections. Memory also works forward (prospective memory), allowing an anticipation of what will happen next, or imagined alternatives, or invented fictional events. Our memories can be vivid, but are almost always temporally imprecise. It is a rare person who can remember what they had for lunch last week, let alone a year ago. It requires effort to recall even a recent film scene by scene, to remember how you felt before you knew the villain was really the hero, and the *dénouement* actually a sting, etc.[99]

As a result, the present looms large and all-consuming to the senses and hogs the limelight in evaluation. Social scientists have conducted experiments to ascertain people's willingness to accept a larger reward later compared to a smaller one now. The results reveal us as a species for whom the future is a hazy and undefined 'not now'. In culture, as in other areas of policy making, it is much easier to get politicians excited about a Shiny Bright Thing than about funding something for future generations. Many of the most important cultural experiences happen because of long-established institutions simply doing their job well long-term. But those institutions are continually required to spend significant effort demonstrating their immediate benefits. How can we improve this faulty and wasteful sense of time passed and time to come?

---

99   For more on the relationship between memory and culture see Julian Meyrick and Katie Cavanagh 'An Unfinished Conversation. Play Texts, Digital Projection, and Dramaturgy'. *Arts and Humanities in Higher Education.* Special Issue, December, 2016. http://www.artsandhumanities.org/journal/an-unfinished-conversation-play-texts-digital-projection-and-dramaturgy/

The Primacy of Narrative

Enter narrative! The stories people tell are far more than handy containers for haphazard facts and feelings. A narrative is a dynamic ordering of information that can cope with time. Built carefully and read critically, it is an essential vehicle in the pursuit of truth. The historian Hayden White has observed that narrative is a device for creating meaning out of what would otherwise be disparate information.[100] Early information conditions the understanding of later information so that narratives act as compounding arcs of understanding that are active, selective and consequential. The challenge today is that constructing meaningful narratives is hard because there is so *much* information to select from. Banish the thought that narrative construction is facile, easy work. It is the most important way of dealing with the welter of evaluative decisions we must make.

The first narratives we tell are ones about ourselves. 'I am the sort of person who ...'; 'I like the kinds of things that ...'; 'I've always wanted to ...'. These kinds of statements are more than one-dimensional expressions of purchasing desire. They reach back to the past to shape our personal history, and stretch out to provide a guide for our future actions. Narratives permit time to be represented in a meaningful way and for our choices to escape the prison of the present. In outline, a narrative is a basic device. It orders information according to a beginning–middle–end pattern, and allows different choices to be related across evaluative registers. While simple enough to be accessible to very young children (stories are among the first things we remember, though it is equally true to say that stories are the first form our memories take), they can also be sophisticated representations of intentions and of complex realities.

---

100 See Hayden White, 'The Value of Narrativity in the Representation of Reality', *Critical Inquiry*, 7.1 (1980), 5–27.

Box 8 'What's the Story?' below gives 10 points about narrative construction and its use in the evaluative process. It is designed to deepen our appreciation of narrative and its extraordinary sense-making power.

Box 8 What's the Story? Guide to Narrating Value

1. **Definitions of narrative** 'A chain of events in a cause–effect relationship occurring in time' (Bordwell & Thompson, *Film Art*, 1980); 'Intentional-communicative artefacts ... that have as their function the communication of a story' (Gregory Currie, *Narratives and Narrators*, 2010); 'The solution to the fundamental problem of our species: how to translate knowing into telling' (Hayden White, *The Routledge Companion to Historical Studies*, 2000).

2. **What is narrative?** An oral, visual, or written account of causally related information (often, connected events), with a subject, a mode, and an object. It has a beginning, middle and an end (though not always in that order!). These are sequentially presented such that their combination is greater than the sum of their parts. A narrative is more than the information contained within it. It offers an understanding, or framework that is sense-making in a holistic way.

3. **How does narrative work?** Narrative works in the minds of its hearers/readers by the sequential release of information so that further degrees of inference become possible. Narratives focus data but do not aggregate it. Instead, they shape it, and allow sophisticated interpretations of the original information presented, which permit a 'going beyond the data'. Being causally related, narratives are useful for reporting on time-flows and time horizons. Because human beings have poor memories for both past events and future consequences, narratives are key mnemonic devices

for organising, retaining and recalling information that fluctuates over time.

4. **How does narrative organise, refer to, and render accessible the real world?** Narrative selects the relevant features of real-world activities and experiences and places them in a simplified model that is causally related. The basic shape of a narrative is 'and now this/and now this/and now this etc.' with each 'this' being linked to the 'this' before and after it. Thus activities and experiences that are not physically observable can be meaningfully evoked and not reduced to an arbitrary series of measurement indices (the fallacy of functionalism). Their origins and driving purposes can also thus be revealed.

5. **How does narrative organise, refer to and render accessible non-narrative information (e.g. statistics)?** Narrative co-exists with non-narrative information. Numbers only 'tell a story' when selected from their tables and connected in ways that narrativise meaning or causation. Quantitative data (tables, graphs, diagrams) can embed in a narrative to provide a single point of focus, or can appear alongside the narrative by way of providing an alternative model of reality. Methods that combine narrative and non-narrative information are well-established in many fields of research, including some of the most resolutely 'evidence-based' fields.

6. **What is 'good' narrative construction?** Narrative construction is 'good' when it speaks clearly to a purpose, to shape and render accessible a wide swathe of source data, encouraging sophisticated interpretation without loss of meaning. This is more than a merely technical skill: good narratives are credible, balanced and ethical. When organising data, narratives should not swamp it or 'spin' it in distorting ways. Instead, they should

conduct a dialogue with data, and the transparency and honesty of that dialogue is central to 'good' narrative construction. Likewise, the type of understanding that narratives offer should be cause for reflection. Narratives are *always* provisional. It is *always* the case that new or different information can alter the spectrum of possible narrative constructions for a dataset. 'Good' narratives don't pretend to be reality. They admit their second-order status as models of reality. They do not over-promote themselves.

7. **Can narratives produce new knowledge or do they merely organise existing knowledge?** By enabling sophisticated interpretation of source data, narratives make new registers of value available, especially in respect of causes and consequences. They also transpose non-narrative data into a more accessible form without loss of meaning. In these ways, narratives are similar to arguments and can produce new knowledge about the objects, relations, events and processes they address.

8. **What are the ethical principles underlying the construction of narratives?** Real-world narratives aim to be credible. There are circumstances in which 'complete' data is unavailable and inference and surmise are unavoidable. But the criterion of credibility is always key. Credibility in narrative comes in various forms. For example, there is the credibility of facts, and the credibility of an interpretation of those facts. The first is a matter of verifiable proposition, the second of plausible explanation. However, the assumption is that when narrative is used as an evaluative technique it is *engaged with the truth* on all levels, and its efficacy and trustworthiness are enhanced by such engagement.

9. **What are the uses of narrative construction in particular situations?** Narratives may be used to explain the origins, trajectory and purpose of a particular institution. Narratives may be used to explain the success or otherwise of an individual project. The decision to communicate and judge 'success' or 'failure' is an evaluative strategy available only through narrative. Narratives may be used to explain the events and outcomes of a given year's activities. Narratives may be used to explain and argue for the *potential* of a certain program, building or event. They can be descriptive or persuasive, and are often a mixture of both.

10. **What are the limits of narratives as a technique?** Narrative is limited by three parameters. First, there is information that does not suit the narrative form because it is not possible to reduce, select and sequentially present it. Second, as a technique, narratives always raise the possibility of counter-narratives. Indeed, this is key to their use as sense-making devices. There is always another story to be told. Finally, narrative is limited by the sophistication of writing and reading skills. Narratives make use of rhetorical devices like metaphor, synecdoche, enthymeme (compressed argument), mood, rhythm, imagery, contrast, personification, repetition, hyperbole and ambiguity. These devices must be used by capable writers and readers to keep on the yellow brick road of truth-telling.

The Rhetorical Economy

As well as framing the things that happen around us and shaping the choices we make, narratives link up to each other. Stories explain other stories, arranging themselves in webs of joined-up intelligence that allow us to quickly assess external events through Kahneman's 'thinking fast' rather than detailed analysis.[101] If you don't like football, you don't have to watch every match in every code to confirm it. If you don't like modern art, it's likely that an exhibition of new young painters will also prove unappealing. Some narratives are little more than an expression of I-like-coffee/you-like-tea personal preference. But others are collective, coercive and large-scale. These kinds of 'grand narratives', as they are called, haven't gone away, even if the term has acquired negative connotations. 'American democracy', 'European unity' and 'Australian multiculturalism' are phrases that go beyond the merely descriptive, soliciting commitments, opinions and, of course, values. 'The free market' is perhaps the most dominant grand narrative of our time. Such words and phrases are not set in stone, but shift constantly and are occasionally subject to explosive and sudden transformation. Think of the meaning of the Berlin Wall before and after its fall.

Some narratives over-determine the shape and the meaning of other narratives. To take a recent and conspicuous example, the extraordinary success of the Museum of Old and New Art in Hobart reflects the value of more than just one gallery and one audience. It is part of a broader account that includes not only the Tasmanian cultural sector but the state's economy and self-image ('the MONA effect'). Narratives lead in a way that numerical data never leads. If you are told that 30,000 people went to MONA last month, you

---

101 see *Thinking, Fast and Slow*, especially Part I.

have heard a story first and quantitative evidence second. The story is supplied by its context. Perhaps you think that 30,000 must be a lot of people to rate a mention; or perhaps it was just that there was a cultural event accessible to a certain number of people, a certain number of whom actually saw it. Data will take you only so far. A future project; a creative process; a long-term cultural practice: these things don't require evidence of the statistical kind so much as a persuasive vision, tacit knowledge, and continued collective acceptance. Evidence is only evidence when a narrative makes it evidence. Only a narrative can say what it is evidence *of.* In 2010 there was no evidence that building MONA – as opposed to another kind of cultural institution, or a new sewage works – would be a beneficial anything. It is hard to imagine a quantitative analysis of public need for which MONA would have been the required solution. But David Walsh's money and vision made it happen, and it works.

This *prospective* aspect of evaluation has a variety of labels: 'vision', 'aspiration', 'mission', 'hope'. It is important to grasp that statements made about the future are not without evidence, but do have a different relationship to it. For example, the goal of 'building a sustainable and successful film industry' is one that can be given targets and tracked only to a degree. To begin with, people will have different ideas about what 'sustainability' and 'success' actually mean, and different measures of it will conflict. Different stories can also be told from the same set of facts. If 10 films are made in a year, and two are outstandingly successful while eight are not, how is this to be measured against a year in which 10 films were averagely received? If shooting Hollywood movies in Australia generates more money than shooting local ones, is that good or bad for Australian cinema? It depends whether making Australian films matters more than making money. And, if so, how much more?

Only a narrative of national identity and/or economic prosperity can make sense of this crucial policy choice.

Finally, narrative as an evaluation strategy requires great care with language, something explored in the previous chapter. Not only do different words mean different things to different people, but the ways certain terms are used by some people, especially governments and experts, affect the ways everyone else uses them. Australian culture occupies a 'rhetorical economy' in which a word like 'excellence' can attract or lose meaning as a precise descriptor. People use it in different contexts without noticing they are only superficially talking about the same thing. If our narratives repeatedly use 'excellence' in this way, we are not elucidating anything specific about an artwork or cultural activity, we are merely claiming a status.

It is hard to imagine a world in which people do not go in for such self-promotion. But too much of this and narrative construction becomes the spin cycle. Words lose their power to say particular things and instead become a kind of background muzak, believable only to those who like the tune. Again, this will be a signal problem for culture that by its nature is multidimensional, complex and controversial. Cultural activities are difficult enough to talk about meaningfully without being loaded up with self-regard. The narrative skills needed for effective participation in the rhetorical economy are thus as exacting as the ones required for statistical compilation or metrical measurement. As a society, narrative skills help us make the journey from an inert, reductive and overly-monetised conception of value – which captures only a few of the choices we have to make – to the larger, richer, and realer realm of *evaluation*.

CHAPTER SEVEN

The Reporting of Value

We speak to the organizer. She asks 'why have you come to Singapore? Isn't there a course in Australia?' She talks about the relative failure of Integrated Reporting in Singapore. She says it didn't have enough grounding in the right values and that, in this respect, Sustainability Reporting is ethically more fundamental than <IR>. We explain our interest in this kind of reporting for the cultural sector. She asks 'what's the cultural sector?', which is not a question we get asked that often! We say 'arts organisations, mostly non-profit'. She says 'being at Bloomberg is not the usual setting for a workshop like this'. Bloomberg is like a trading floor from a Hollywood financial disaster movie – screens everywhere, free food and drink, harassed workers glued to screens with little coloured bar charts that bob up and down, numbers flitting past like neutrinos. Nothing says 'sustainability'. Everything says 'profit'.

> Notes on a Sustainability Reporting Workshop. Sept 2016,
> Bloomberg, Singapore.

Ticking the Boxes

In Laboratory Adelaide, every time we step into the public arena we get asked about our 'methodology'. People are keen, even desperate, for a way to validate their belief that culture matters.

But methodology alone will not do this work. This does not mean our view on arts funding is 'just hand over the money and bugger off'. That would be both elitist and anti-democratic. So this chapter begins a discussion about what a better relationship between cultural practitioners and their supporters might look like. The answer lies in more meaningful value reporting.

What do all parts of the cultural sector have in common? The answer is banal: they are constantly describing and justifying what they do to other parts. In previous centuries this meant writing to rich patrons (e.g. Samuel Johnson's hostile letter to Lord Chesterfield, 1755), seeking audiences with powerful monarchs (e.g. Moliere's with Louis XIV in the 1660s), and making public arguments and apologias (e.g. Virginia Woolf's *A Room of One's Own*, 1929). Such things still happen, but in Western societies, and in the rapidly developing BRIC ones (Brazil, Russia, India and China), these activities have largely been replaced by one so ubiquitous it seems almost beneath notice: filling in forms.

Artists and cultural organisations fill in forms for many reasons: to apply for a grant; to claim a tax exemption; to request a license to perform or sell goods; to comply with occupational health and safety requirements; to insure themselves, their audiences or their art; to take their work abroad; to explain their work to a particular community or regulatory body. The list goes on and on. The forms they fill in are not bespoke. Forms are not designed to capture everything about something, but something about everything. To do this they break down complex real-world phenomena into a series of blank informational categories. Obvious ones include 'name', 'address' and 'occupation'. This kind of data is basic and iterative. We spend a good portion of our lives relaying it over and over, in slightly different ways. Sometimes this information takes a verbal form, sometimes numerical. Occasionally, as with passports and driver's licences, visual material is required also. The ordinariness of forms is deceptive. The fact that much of the information they solicit is old, repetitive or redundant is designed to reveal opposite traits: what is new, different and divergent. The modern form is a searchlight, aimed at distinguishing between what is unremarkable and always required ('mandatory information'), what is relevant to a particular situation or occasion ('eligibility criteria') and what is to be weighed in the balance and awarded, rewarded, censured or rejected. The whole process – the form (physical or online), the social interactions around it, the decisions it facilitates and the consequences of those decisions – we can call 'reporting'. In arts and culture, as elsewhere, it has low status. 'Ticking the boxes' is a refrain that can be frequently heard from the sector, in tones of resignation or plangent complaint. Dreary, time-consuming, useless, removed: reporting is the soul-deadening price to be paid for engaging in arts and culture themselves, which are, by contrast, exciting, technicoloured and fun.

But what if reporting wasn't like that? What if it was an engaged, serious, and purposeful activity that reflected more of culture's worth because it was more worthwhile itself? What if the endless forms we have to fill in were a chance for artists and cultural organisations to speak meaningfully about what they do?

In 2015, the Laboratory Adelaide researchers met the author Jane Gleeson-White, who had just published *Six Capitals: The Revolution Capitalism Has to Have – or Can Accountants Save the Planet?* She is both an art historian and an accountant. Her book introduces the lay reader to new reporting reforms in the corporate world that seek to change the way companies both write their annual reports, and, more broadly, the way they talk about what they contribute (or not) to the global polity. She writes:

> Many at the forefront of corporate reporting believe that in
> the future we will not be talking about reporting at all; we

will be talking about corporate *communication*. Reporting is an industry-style, one-way process from a company to give information to the mass of its shareholders. By contrast, communication is a multi-directional form of relating and can encompass individual exchanges between the company and those with a stake in its activities ... [P]roponents of integrated reporting believe that integrated thinking and reporting can shift the focus of managers and investors to the long term. And because of the power of corporations, the future of the planet depends on it.[102]

As result of meeting Gleeson-White, Laboratory Adelaide developed an interest in two innovative corporate reporting approaches or 'frameworks': the Global Reporting Initiative (GRI) and Integrated Reporting (<IR>). These are complex areas of accounting theory and practice, and we do not claim to be proficient in them. On the other hand, both frameworks are designed in part for non-expert use. Their emphasis on *communication* exemplifies the points we want to make in respect of language and narrative. We sketch their main points of interest for cultural practitioners who should, we suggest, set aside their low opinion of reporting and explore a way to move forward a discussion about value stuck in 'economic impact mode' since the 1980s.

Neither GRI nor <IR> are silver bullet solutions to the challenges the cultural sector faces. And they have problems of their own, a main one being the competing tension between reporting financial and non-financial forms of value. This is reflected in the quote at the top of this section, taken from our notes when we attended sustainability report training ourselves in 2016. Nor do GRI or <IR> provide slick suites of app-like 'tools'. They have methods but are not defined by them. They are more properly described

---

102 Gleeson-White, *Six Capitals*, 227.

as holistic evaluative systems designed to focus thinking on what matters. They are expressions of a reporting reform looking beyond reporting, to the assumptions and behaviour they describe and justify. By articulating new forms of value via these frameworks, we can articulate new forms of value in our lives.

The next few pages give a brief introduction to these approaches to value. Those who like detail will discover there is plenty of detail on GRI and <IR> to be had, allowing sophisticated judgment about their strengths, limitations, uptake, formal modelling and so forth (see the Appendix which gives the relevant web links). However, after two years acquaintance with the frameworks we believe there are some key aspects that should be highlighted when considering their applicability for culture.

First, they are principles-based rather than rules-governed. Neither GRI nor <IR> supply a 'one size fits all' template for every organisation, but seek to turn reporting into an exercise in real knowledge transmission. Their principles, which we will touch on in a moment, are the opposite of 'boxes to be ticked'. They are commitments designed to elicit a deeper response from organisations about the issues *they themselves* think are important. There are mandatory information fields, of course (GRI calls them 'universal standards'). But there are also fields that are selective and elective (GRI calls them 'topic specific standards') that apply to particular sectors and to particular organisations that identify with them.

This highlights a third feature of the frameworks: they are not coercive. They ask companies to report 'in accordance with' their principles or, a lesser degree, to 'reference' them. Even in those countries that mandate sustainability reporting (like Singapore) or integrated reporting (like South Africa), the emphasis is less on compliance than internalisation. Both frameworks allow a phased approach, indeed encourage it, so that the principles are adopted meaningfully rather than in a speedy but superficial way. Such gradualism also facilitates a fourth distinguishing feature of these frameworks: their interest in properly aligning numerical and non-numerical information. There is use of quantitative indicators and targets in both GRI and <IR>, but these metrics draw their sense from the qualitative information arranged around them. During our own sustainability report training, we were asked to look at a Nestlé company report. We went straight to the numerical data, but were told sternly, 'don't be driven by the data; stand above the data; if you go straight to the data, you won't get the whole picture; you will have "an answer" before you know what the question is. You won't know if you are looking at everything you should be.'

'Everything' for GRI and <IR> is the world of value beyond financial return. The ethical impulse behind the approaches comes from the environmental movement, and the belief that capitalism is in danger of exhausting the planet's resources, degrading its labour force, and discounting all that isn't profit in the pockets of shareholders. The reduction of value to financial value is unacceptable for two reasons. First, because corporations are given special privileges by the modern state, that mean they should consider the public interest and not just their own. Second, because non-financial forms of value are increasingly important in an economy where natural, social and intellectual (and we would argue cultural) sources of wealth add greatly to successful and sustainable living.

Finally, binding all these interests together is a bigger and more dynamic sense of time than in traditional accounting. GRI is focused on intergenerational equity; <IR> on how value is created over short, medium and long terms. With both frameworks, there is a clear sense of what organisations need to get away from – a chronic and debilitating short-termism, a hyper-focus on 'the now' of the current financial reporting period at the expense of the costs and benefits that become evident when other time frames are considered. While much of the GRI and <IR> literature is concerned with capturing environmental, social and governance activity and bringing it into a 'value matrix', what makes the exercise real and rewarding is a richer view of time. This is crucial for arts and culture, whose value often appears slowly, over years, or even generations, as many of the examples in this book show.

GRI Described

As GRI and <IR>'s commentators Robert Eccles and Michael Krzus stress, these frameworks spring from what is at heart a social movement.[103] As such, they are examples of regulatory responses to the failures of corporate capitalism in the post-communist era. The King Report on Governance for South Africa (King III), which in 2011 mandated <IR> for all companies listed on the Johannesburg Stock Exchange on an 'apply or explain' basis, is a moment of origin for <IR>.[104] It occurred within a wave of global interest in reforming corporate reporting practices that included the UK Companies Act 2006, and the Danish Financial Statement Act 2008. GRI, established in 1997, is older than <IR>. The California-based Sustainability Accounting Standards Board, known for its rigorous assessment methodology, was established in 2011. The UK-based Carbon Disclosure Project appeared in 2001 and is linked to the Climate Disclosure Standards Board, founded in 2007. All these bodies focus on 'triple bottom line reporting' or Environmental, Social and Governance (ESG) indices. Above them all sits the

---

103 Robert Eccles and Michael Krzus, *One Report: Integrated Reporting for a Sustainable Strategy* (Hoboken, NJ: Wiley & Sons, 2010).

104 See information from the Institute of South African Directors, at www.iodsa. co.za/?kingIII.

UN's 17 sustainable development goals, of which, it should be noted, cultural development is *not* one.

How does GRI work? As said above, it encourages a phased approach. Companies do not suddenly start reporting on sustainability. Usually they adopt a three-year rollout, with emphasis on quality and specificity of reporting. The framework links reporting topics to metrics in a way that assists proper contextualisation, and the pertinent articulation of the intentions and directions of an organisation. Different reporting standards exist for different industrial sectors. Within each topic-specific standard, there are disclosures that are required, disclosures that are recommended, and guidelines for the provision of discretionary information. The commitment is to an 'improvement cycle', to reporting, over time, reflecting GRI principles more deeply, thus encouraging better real-world behaviour. The advantage of a phased approach is that it gives both report writers and report readers time to grasp the advantages of holistic communication. Choice of metrics is a last step. Because there is flexibility in specific standards, there is flexibility in quantitative indicators. The two work together – words and numbers – to create a useful, trustworthy, and credible report.

Sustainability is about more than using low-energy light bulbs and recycled toilet paper. It is, in the words of PAIA, a GRI-training company, 'about risk management in the broader sense'.[105] It has an inter-generational focus, ensuring our children and grandchildren inherit the planet in as good a condition as we experience it now. Many things can damage this legacy: resource depletion, economic inequality, social injustice, declining health and wellbeing, and low educational standards. GRI records corporate impacts in all these domains and encourages their mitigation. Christopher Davis, the

---

105 See paiaconsulting.com.sg/sustainability-training/.

Body Shop's CEO, put it neatly and with the right moral emphasis: 'sustainability is about being a little less awful'.[106]

Given its broad understanding of value, GRI is particularly concerned with 'intangibles', the wealth we generate beyond hard cash and material goods. Non-financial information is at the crux of what makes sustainability reporting new. While there is no doubting the ethical roots of GRI, its adoption into business models is driven by changing fiscal realities as well. One is the increasing interconnectedness of the global economy, so that sustainability performance is now closely related to stock market price. For example, a badly run mine in Papua New Guinea can damage BHP's share price in Sydney and London. Another is the shifting ratio between tangible and intangible wealth. In 1975, 17 per cent of a company's capital value typically lay in intangible assets. In 1995, it was 68 per cent. In 2015, it was 84 per cent.[107] The world has changed, and our perceptions of the world along with it. For example, Facebook lost trust and share value in 2018 for not having guarded its personal data better from unscrupulous data-miners. Developments in economic theory, public interest in 'legacy effects', and the speed with which opinions can be shared on the internet mean that value looks very different in the corporate realm than it did 30 or even 10 years ago.

The key principles of GRI report **content** are as follows:[108] *sustainability context* (a report should be 'presented in the wider context of ... how an organisation contributes, or aims to contribute to areas of focus in sustainability'); *materiality* (a report should 'reflect an organisation's significant economic, environmental and

---

106 See *The Economist*, 'In the Thicket of it', 8 July 2016.

107 See Ocean Tomo Report at www.oceantomo.com/blog/2015/03-05-ocean-tomo-2015-intangible-asset-market-value/.

108 Following content and quotations based on PAIA materials supplied for workshop; see paiaconsulting.com.sg/sustainability-training/.

social impacts'); *stakeholder inclusiveness* (a report should 'identify [an organisation's] stakeholders, and explain how it has responded to their reasonable expectations and interests'); and *completeness* ('encompasses the dimensions of scope, boundary and time').

The key principles of GRI report **quality** are as follows: *balance* (a report 'should reflect positive and negative aspects of the organisation's performance'); *comparability* (a report 'should be presented in a manner that enables stakeholders to analyze changes in the organization's performance over time, and ... relative to other organizations'); *accuracy* ('information should be sufficiently accurate and detailed for stakeholders to assess [an] organization's performance'); *timeliness* ('refers both to the regularity of reporting as well as its proximity to the actual events described'); *clarity* ('information [should be] available in a manner that is understandable and accessible to stakeholders'); and *reliability* ('stakeholders should have confidence that a report can be checked to establish the veracity of its contents').

These principles are ones of good faith and 'black and white' communication (no hiding bad news!). An organisation's narrative is obviously primary. GRI asks organisations to report on what they believe to be relevant and significant, and this has to be done discursively before it is shown metrically. At the same time, GRI's widening of focus from shareholders to stakeholders means narrative has to do more than relay information about the value an organisation is accruing to itself. It must describe and justify what good it is doing in the world, what value it is providing to others.

\<IR\> Described

Of the relationship between GRI and \<IR\>, Eccles and Krzus comment that the former 'provides a strong foundation' for the latter, while they 'differ little in terms of their primary audience'.[109] The International Integrated Reporting Council (IIRC) was founded in 2009, and like GRI makes its terms and guidelines freely available. A document published in 2014 defines integrated thinking as 'the active consideration by an organization of the relationships between its various operating and functional units and the capitals that the organization uses or affects'. Integrated reporting is 'a process founded on integrated thinking that results in a periodic integrated report by an organization about value creation over time', and an integrated report is

> a concise communication about how an organisation's strategy, governance, performance and prospects, in the context of its external environment, lead to the creation of value over the short, medium and long term.[110]

<IR> shares many of the principles of GRI but, as is clear from these remarks, puts great stress on *connectivity* between different types of information, and value-generation over time. Connectivity is a function of simplicity and concision, and this is a pain point for a framework that aims to produce *one* report that overarches any others an organisation might generate. It is hard not hear a version of the central refrain from *Lord of the Rings*: 'One report to rule them all, one report to bind them/One report to bring them all and in a value matrix bind them'. The more information a report tries to integrate, the more complex it becomes, and the less effective it is as a communication tool. It may seem counterintuitive, but often the best thing a report can do is provide *less* information (we would argue especially quantitative information) so that what is presented is more accessible and interpretable. Often reports feel like the terms and conditions on an internet purchase – deliberately lengthy

---

109 Eccles and Krzus, *One Report*, 71.
110 Eccles and Krzus, *One Report*, 71.

and opaque to discourage readers from discovering salient detail. Use of 'white space' in a report is not necessarily absence of data. It can be room to think.

At the heart of the <IR> framework are its six different categories of wealth or 'capitals': financial, manufactured, intellectual, human, social and relationship, and natural (for this reason, it is sometimes called 'the capitals approach'). The IIRC notes, 'not all capitals are equally relevant or applicable to all organizations'.[111] The capitals exist 'as a guideline to ensure the organization does not overlook a capital that it uses or affects'.[112] The capitals are inputs. The value creation process is what happens to the capitals after they are turned into first outputs, then outcomes. As with GRI, value creation is dynamic and reflexive. The IIRC comment, 'the value creation process is not static; regular review of each component and its interactions with other components, and a focus on the organization's *outlook*, lead to revision and refinement to improve all the components'.[113] In other words, an organisation's value is related to an organisation's vision. We are back to narrative again, with the importance of binding disparate information into a report that can cope with the flux of time, and the fact that, as human beings, we have such limited perception of the future.

Where could culture fit into the <IR> framework? Three of its capitals deal with tangible assets (financial, manufactured, and natural) and three with intangible ones (intellectual, human, social and relationship). Aspects of culture are reflected across the six categories, but its more immanent qualities – its inherent, aesthetic, or 'cultural' value, as well as its less overt psychological and social

---

111 See *The International <IR> Framework*, 2.16: integratedreporting.org/
     wp-content/uploads/2015/03/13-12-08-THE-INTERNATIONAL-IR-
     FRAMEWORK-2-1.pdf.
112 *The International <IR> Framework*, 2.19.
113 *The International <IR> Framework*, 2.29 (original emphasis).

effects – could be listed under intellectual capital ('knowledge-based intangibles'), human capital ('people's competencies and experience; their motivation to innovate'), or social and relationship capital ('ability to share information to enhance individual and collective well-being'). A more radical proposal would be to add a seventh category to the <IR> foundational list: cultural capital. Certainly, the <IR> framework is flexible enough to incorporate such a move and embed culture in a way that would allow explicit acknowledgment of its value.

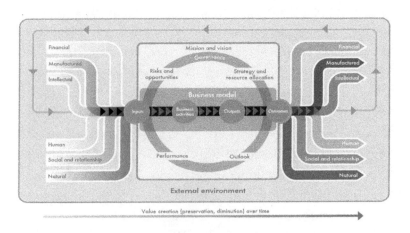

Figure 1: The Value Creation Process in the <IR> Framework, showing the six input capitals ("the Octopus model"). We propose Culture added as a **seventh capital**.
Source: The International <IR> Framework (2013): P. 13

Reporting Principles for Culture?

There are exciting possibilities in GRI and <IR>. Many of the benefits arising from cultural activity are hard to articulate in quantitative, especially monetised terms. This leaves three ways forward. First, by developing quantitative measures of non-quantitative value. This is the approach taken by so-called 'quality metrics', like Western Australia's Culture Counts dashboard system. Such a tactic is fraught with problems, both methodological and political, and Laboratory Adelaide has written about these at length elsewhere.[114] Second, by rejecting all quantification as skewed towards instrumentalism and/or financial value, and using qualitative assessment methods alone. This seems unlikely to prevail in a data-fixated society such as ours, where quantitative information is akin to Linus's blanket in the *Peanuts* cartoons. Besides, numbers usually tell us something of value about value, even if they fall short of the total picture. A third avenue is to combine both types of information in a way that makes sense of them as different but aligned sources of knowledge. This is GRI and <IR>'s promise for culture. But there is also promise in culture for these reporting frameworks, for the kind of values that cultural organisations generate are predominantly intangible as traditional accounting views them. They are, consequently, varied and interesting enough to enrich thinking about organisational communication. Reporting reform and culture are natural allies, and a closer relationship between them could be conceptually and practically fruitful in both fields.

If we put the issues raised in this chapter together – sustainability, integration, financial and non-financial information, tangible and intangible wealth, and time – the problem of culture's value appears in a new light. We can stop talking about 'methodology' in

---

114 See particularly Robert Phiddian, Julian Meyrick, Tully Barnett and Richard Maltby, 'Counting Culture to Death: An Australian Perspective on Culture Counts and Quality Metrics', *Cultural Trends*, 26.2 (2017), 174–80.

a simplistic sense. Metrical methods may play a part in supplying evidence of culture's social and economic effects. But culture's value is something that arises from the operation of a complex system and it is the system that deserves our attention, not just certain designated proxies. A measure of value is only as good as the reporting relationships in which it is embedded. When these relationships aren't grounded in a meaningful understanding of what culture is, trust is lost and no set of numbers will get it back. The presenter in Singapore explained to us that: 'one of the great strengths of the GRI is that it doesn't try to reinvent anything. It has no ego. If there is something out there that works, it doesn't try to replace it. It works with it and assists it'. This is crucial to extending the reporting reform to culture. GRI and <IR> do not ask cultural practitioners to replace what they do, the numbers they crunch, the stories they tell. They ask them to reappraise their effectiveness and meaning in light of wider environmental, social and governance goals – goals they will overwhelmingly share. The frameworks encourage organisations to consider all the benefits they provide to the community: to consider value in the deepest sense. We should not be over-optimistic. Changing economic and political habits is, in the words of Max Weber, 'a slow boring through hard boards'. However, there are opportunities in both reporting frameworks. Their conception of time is different – it is longer term. Their conception of benefit is different – it is broader, stakeholder-based and includes intangible assets. Their conception of reporting is different – it is narratively-driven and uses metrics where they support the qualitative vision an organisation is trying to communicate. In other words, the aim of these frameworks is not information but understanding. Providing information is key to talking meaningfully about the value of arts and culture. But achieving understanding is a prior and more profound task to providing information.

What might a set of reporting principles look like for culture? In 2016, we had a stab at drafting just such a document. Like GRI and <IR> we imagined not a coercive set of rules, but voluntary protocols to which practitioners would subscribe as a means of improving their own reporting – of going beyond 'ticking the boxes'. We reproduce it here as an example of how a new reporting framework for culture might be anchored in six principles of meaningful communication.

Box 9 Charter of Cultural Reporting: Six Principles of Meaningful Communication

PRINCIPLE 1: COMMITMENT TO SENSE MAKING
- Be timely.
- Be in good faith.
- Be meaningful to all stakeholders.
- Be concise.
- Acknowledge context.
- Acknowledge assumptions.
- Be relevant, representative and readable.

PRINCIPLE 2: COMMITMENT TO A REPORTING RELATIONSHIP
- Reports are ultimately a communication 'person to person'.
- Reports involve a context on both the side of those writing them and those reading them.
- Reports have a general function but must be critically meaningful about the activities they report on.
- Reports exist in a spectrum of other communication acts which support them.
- Reports manage and promote trust, but are not a substitute for it.
- Reports are not a substitute for cultural experience itself, and a minimum amount of actual contact with art and culture is necessary from readers for reports to be understandable at all.

PRINCIPLE 3: COMMITMENT TO PLAIN LANGUAGE
- Reports should use language to describe, explain and justify in equal measure.
- Reports should use words with evident meaning and application, and explain specialised terms.
- Reports should not define words outside their common usage and, where possible, seek to inform that usage rather than determine it.
- Reports should avoid over-using abstract terms – especially adjectives and adverbs repurposed as nouns.

PRINCIPLE 4: COMMITMENT TO COMMUNICATING ALL TYPES OF VALUE CREATION
- Reports should distinguish between different types of value creation, not just different degrees of it.
- Reports should clearly communicate different time periods in value creation in the past and the future, especially the short and long term.
- Reports should acknowledge all stakeholders in the value creation process.
- Reports should distinguish between indeterminacy (things that cannot be known) and deliberate artistic risk (that is know to some extent) in the value creation process.

PRINCIPLE 5: COMMITMENT TO IMPROVED INTEGRATION OF QUANTITATIVE AND QUALITATIVE INFORMATION
- Quantitative indicators should be embedded in qualitative accounts, not the other way round.
- Quantitative indicators should be contextualised and interpreted in the report, and that interpretation should strive to be true, fair and complete.
- Quantitative indicators should aspire to indicate a variety of types of value.

- Quantitative indicators should be adequately explained in terms of the qualitative relations that they stand proxy for.

PRINCIPLE 6: COMMITMENT TO REPORTING ON THE MEANING OF CULTURE, NOT JUST ITS ECONOMIC AND SOCIAL EFFECTS
- Show respect for artists.
- Show respect for government and other funders.
- Acknowledge that culture is an artistic activity, not just a social function.
- Acknowledge the role and perspective of the audience, spectator, reader, co-participant etc.
- Acknowledge the risk, difficulty and unpredictability of culture's value to the society that supports it.

Conclusion

Over the four years of Laboratory Adelaide's life we have followed debates about value wherever these have led us. We have talked to artists, academics, economists, CEOs, consultants, statisticians and artists again. Our conclusion is that government policy has reached a strange moment when quantitative measures have achieved dominant power over the least quantifiable area of human endeavour – culture. If that were all, it would be serious enough, but the inadequacy of such methods for assessing culture is only a symptom of a deeper failure to articulate *what matters* in many domains. Why? Answering a question of this magnitude inevitably involves speculation. But Laboratory Adelaide has these thoughts to offer by way of concluding our short book.

Thought 1: Not Everything That Counts Can Be Counted

There's an old joke about some tourists who get lost in the countryside, and stop at a farm to ask for directions. 'Well, if I were you', the farmer tells them sagely, 'I wouldn't be starting from here.' Historically and geographically, we are where we are in the value debate. Periods and places have their outlooks and ideas, which are invariably presented as if they are facts of nature. Whether the ideas are political, philosophical, legal, scientific or culinary, they constitute 'the background', the assumed knowledge we use on a daily basis. Like any background, their fixative power arises from the fact we don't notice them much. That is not necessarily invidious. If we had to constantly reflect on the structure of our own thinking, there would be no time for doing anything else. Perhaps it is enough to trust that, when the moment comes, ideas that have outworn their welcome will wither in open debate.

Or perhaps it isn't. As the joke above suggests, some ideas are just no place to start. Flawed in themselves, they also block better ideas. So it is with the contemporary belief that anything can be measured. Or to be accurate, with the belief that anything can be *meaningfully* measured, that a metric can be generated for all objects, events, relations and processes, and that these can be ordered in statistical graphs and tables to show the truth of the phenomena under examination. In this way, numbers assume the numinous, indwelling logic they had in the days of the Pythagorean brotherhood, back in the sixth century BCE. If our desired destination is proper public discussion about arts and culture, then the sign beside our farm reads 'Shire of Metrical Overreach'. A big part of the issue is the wrong approaches being peddled for the wrong problems. Thus rationality becomes rationalisation, a skein of consistency and sense laundering what is often no more than prejudice and gut feeling.[115] The recent decision by Arts Council England to adopt a 'quality metrics' dashboard is but the latest attempt to numberise aspects of culture that do not lend themselves to any quantitative index. Its Manchester pilot claimed it was:

> very clear that 'excellence' as an outcome measure is
> definable as an absolute standard ('the best of its type
> anywhere') … Taken together, the dashboard of measures
> [we] have generated for the quality of creative product and
> experience (and indeed for quality of creative process and
> cultural leadership) constitutes a rigorous and robust way
> of measuring 'excellence' across the arts and cultural sector
> … It is comparatively easy to see how the dashboard of
> measures suggested scan effectively against the evaluation

---

115 For a deeper account of metric overreach, see Jerry Muller, *The Tyranny of Metrics* (Princeton: Princeton University Press, 2018).

requirements of key public funders (including ACE and local authorities) and major trusts and foundations.[116]

The last point is the not-so hidden catch: ease of government use. At the front is a ridiculous statement about absolute standards. '[T]he best of its type anywhere' begs all the questions it pretends to foreclose. Unless 'type' is defined so narrowly as to be vacuous, the tendentiousness of the approach is hard to distinguish from outright cultural imperialism. More than other areas of life, culture reflects the diversity of society, and the plurality of expressions of which we are all capable. To evaluate even a portion of this is the work of a lifetime. People spend years as film critics, book reviewers, art historians, and musicologists, to mention only the most obvious and traditional of assessment roles. Distinctions between different kinds of cultural offerings, of which the most basic is between 'good' and 'bad', are both arduous and mutable. Culture does not stay still, nor does it upgrade in the way that our computers and washing machines do. Culture in the twenty-first century is not better than culture in the fourteenth century, though it is certainly different. There are no common categories we can use to rank the value of a Castilian polyphonic motet against the value of a funk dance flash-mob, and asking a random sample of people to score them on a Likert scale tells us little about either. Faced with this multiplicity, it is depressing when those charged with 'managing' culture seek to retreat into the simplicity numbers seem to represent. The reality that not everything that counts can be counted is lost in the push to reduce the variety of culture down to bureaucratic formulae claiming to demonstrate that excellence (or innovation or access etc.) has been achieved.

---

116 John Knell, *Manchester Metrics Pilot: Final Report of Stage One*, 2013, 31: www.artscouncil.org.uk/sites/default/files/download-file/Manchester_Metrics_Stage_One_Report_Dec_2013.docx

Forcing important questions of value into a narrow methodological register is both damaging and politically suspect. It is context – historical, social and political – which numbers are apt to leave out. In our overweening desire for benchmarks, KPIs, output variables, and other paraphernalia of 'evidence-based, decision-making' what is lost is the big picture that makes such data meaningful in the first place. A measure of value is mistaken for a means of acknowledging it. This seems to be the awareness behind the Myer, Keir and Fairfax foundations' philanthropic collaboration when they sought tenders for 'A New Approach for Australia's Cultural Sector' in 2016 and put $1.65 million on the table. A new approach to questions of value, not just a better algorithm, is indeed what we need.[117]

But culture is only a limit case, and many other areas of public life are suffering similarly. Talking with a labour economist about the erosion of the Great Barrier Reef, one of the world's greatest natural resources, we were asked, 'but what input price would you put on that?' It is a question both absurd and morally culpable. There is no 'input price' for the Great Barrier Reef because it cannot be replaced by a good of similar kind, or reduced to a money amount with which to compensate people (including, somehow, people in the future), for its irrevocable loss. Our environment is full of 'non-renewables' and culture's objects are often similarly fragile. Their value does not scale numerically. Two mediocre online role-playing games do not add up to one good online role-playing game. Twelve pieces of music remain twelve separate musical experiences. If they cohere into a bigger whole, it is through absorption into an entirely different conception of order – 'an album' or 'a body of work'. Our experiences of culture, like our experiences of the natural world, remain indefeasible.

---

117 See www.humanities.org.au/advice/projects/current/new-approach-program/.

Again, why does culture get treated in this unilluminating and unreal way? The problem arises from our impoverished sense of value that offers little by way of inner resonance to guide judgment beyond the shallow arbitration of consumer choice. The problem crosses many scholarly disciplines. But it is very urgent. If we value only what can easily (i.e. cheaply and accessibly) be counted, we will slight everything that cannot. And much of that everything is what matters in culture. How can the problem be addressed?

Thought 2: A (post-)Functionalist Society?

Ever since the eighteenth and nineteenth centuries brought a utilitarian creed to the fore of public policy-making ('the greatest good for the greatest number'), Western populations have lived in increasingly functionalist societies. In such systems, the value of things is equated with the useful effects they produce, with their practical contribution to a differentiated social order: with their *function*. From iPads to igloos, road signs to rumpus rooms, pacemakers to skyscrapers, function (with its dominant metaphor of the machine) determines the worth of everything. And if this is not how people feel – thinking, for example, that a certain building is *ugly*, or a new phone service *unnecessary* – then that view has to be argued out in functional terms or dismissed as purely personal taste.

It is not just things that attract this evaluative view. People do also. In a functionalist society, you are what you do, and when you stop doing it – through illness, unemployment, or retirement – you cease to matter. You no longer perform your function; or you are downgraded – as disabled, jobless or ageing individuals, labels that mark some as 'leaners' in a society that valorises 'lifters'. In this way, people are reduced to things with functional outcomes. Alternative ways of valuing are not entirely vanquished, of course. They remain at the edges of our social vision – the religious, moral and civic codes that guided us in days gone by, and retain a vestigial presence as 'ghosts in the machine'. They can have a mitigating effect, as when people feel that the way banks behave is 'just plain wrong'. But rarely do they have a dominant voice.

The central operating principle of a functionalist society, its chief manoeuvre, is substitution. In the modern world, everything is replaceable by something else, from pagodas to prime ministers. There is nothing *absolute*, and the relativism that results from this is less moral than administrative. The assumption is that if something or someone in our lives doesn't 'work', doesn't perform the role we expect of them, then we can put something or someone in their place. This gives rise to a logic of substitution that is independent of any particular reasons people have for making a particular switch. Replacement is simply *what we do*, always looking for something that is better, faster, cheaper, cooler, or merely different. We don't repair clothing or appliances because it is easier to buy new ones. This is in part because many related costs – economists' 'externalities' – are left out of the evaluation process: the '$200 hamburger' retails for $9 at the point of consumption.[118]

Living in a functionalist world according to a logic of substitution is not something that keeps most people awake at night, though it does spark some to political dissent and religious revulsion. We mostly become aware of it when we are subject to a functional operation: when we are made redundant in a 'management restructure'; when we are deemed 'an undesirable alien'; when our home is subject to compulsory purchase 'for any purpose in respect of which the Parliament has power to make laws', as the Australian Constitution has it. In these instances, we are the target of a cognate functional procedure: *reclassification*. Subject to different criteria,

---

118 See Raj Patel, *The Value of Nothing: How to Reshape Market Society and Redefine Democracy* (New York: Picador, 2009); see also rajpatel.org/.

we acquire a different social definition, and the whole way we are valued changes. We may feel that we are still the same person, that we have not *done* anything different. But our lives are upended nevertheless through a change in functional status.

Such functionalism provides many benefits, especially material ones. Some, perhaps even many, things suit such a substitutive approach. But some things do not, and it is a particularly bad fit for culture. Here we need an alternative evaluative strategy, one that is not simply another method of counting but a different way of seeing and understanding, built round different operational principles. So what might these be? A central one must be *purpose*. To look at things and people in terms of their *purpose* is to cast them in a wider frame of reference than just consideration of their useful effects. Thus we attend to their aims, missions, visions and hopes – their whole 'world': all the factors that are left out of a functionalist approach to value.

The recent return of aggressive political populism has given salve to those alienated by functional ideas. A technocrat sees only irrationality in the Trump presidency and the Brexit referendum. But they are bad answers to real questions. It is time to imagine a 'post-functionalist' society; a society where function contributes to, but no longer defines and limits, ideas of what matters.[119]

This is a Big Thought, and takes some digesting. A post-functionalist society is not one in which function is irrelevant. It is one that looks beyond useful effects as the sole mark of value. It is one that factors in the broader picture and the longer term. This requires close attention to narrative as well as data, to purpose as well as method. Holism and credibility rather than detail and demonstrative proof must shape our evaluative strategies. A driving

---

119   See Paul Mason, *Postcapitalism: A Guide to Our Future* (London: Allen Lane, 2015) is one extensive guide to what this might look like.

question must be 'What is something *for?*' not just 'Where's the profit?' In moving away from an outmoded functionalism, from a morally deplorable and socially selfish 'Who cares?', we should move towards an engaged and engaging 'What matters?'

Arts and culture are good domains to do this kind of blue skies thinking because they fit substitutive logic so poorly. After all, a life in the arts is driven more by a sense of vocation than a desire to rationally optimise employment options. It is a value in itself. Treating it as a functional choice misses the point – replacing culture's market value for its public value, its consumer impact for its civic influence. To grapple with the problem of culture's value, as an artist, audience or administrator, is to grapple with the problem of value *per se*. This has the potential to be politically transformative at a critical time. So below are some cues for further thought.

Questions to Ask of Evidence-based Approaches

- Is the quantitative data available valid and pertinent evidence for the purpose?
- How much of the experience analysed does the collectable evidence speak to? (i.e. is it a good, bad, or indifferent proxy of value?)
- Does it force quantification of things that are not readily or validly quantifiable?
- What is the opportunity cost of gathering the quantitative data? (i.e. is what it can tell us worth the trouble and expense of gathering it?)
- Will it tell us anything we don't yet know but need to know?
- What practical, political, and marketing uses will the quantitative data be put to?

- Will it lead to a situation where people are likely to manipulate numbers-based evidence as an end in themselves (i.e. game the metrics to gain a 'strategic' advantage)?
- Does the pursuit of commensurability erode meaningful judgement?
- If we decide that it is appropriate to use this quantitative indicator or data collection, do we need to include it every time, in every year, every report, every articulation of value?

Thought 3: Sticking with the Problem (of Value)

Recently, Laboratory Adelaide approached a senior public servant with a proposal for a roundtable discussion with administrators, academics and artists on the value of culture. She was enthusiastic about the panel make-up – but not the topic. We needed to 'move on', she argued, as we 'have talked about the problem of value on a daily basis'. In culture it is probably true to say that anxiety about this is at the forefront of everybody's mind. But are we all talking about the same thing? And are we talking about it *well*? The implication of the conversation was that the debate was exhausted and the 'players' should now talk about something else. But the problem of value is not a three-year university research project. It's not something that can be addressed as a matter of bureaucratic procedure, and certainly not resolved that way. It lies at the heart of every experience in arts and culture. Rather than trying to methodologise the problem away, it is question of living with it better.

The historian of science and theorist of the human condition Donna Haraway has written about *not* moving on from difficult things. She asks, 'what happens when human exceptionalism and bounded individualism, those old saws of Western philosophy and political economics, become unthinkable in the best sciences, whether natural or social? Seriously unthinkable: not available to think with.'[120] She is talking about species and organisms, but the warning is pertinent to other domains. Is our philosophically eroded, politically manipulated understanding of *value* a concept now unavailable to 'think with' in the contemporary moment? Rather than shirking this confronting thought, we should ponder its consequences more deeply. Haraway argues that 'Our task is [also] ... to stir up potent responses to devastating events, as well as to ... rebuild quiet places'.[121]

Much of the value of culture inheres in one sort of trouble or another. Homer starts the *Iliad* with the rage of Achilles, and culture today grapples with the fury of marginalised and affronted groups and classes. Questions of value circulate, but they do not go away. How can we be *attentive* to the problem of value in culture, and beyond culture?

Thought 4: Crisis? What Crisis?

It is easy to claim we face a crisis of value. Perhaps it is a statement that is always true. Nevertheless, a crisis is what Laboratory Adelaide feels it has walked into. When we began in 2014, our only aim was to contribute to the way South Australian artists, cultural organisations and governments talk about what they do, and to extend the national policy conversation beyond a limited creative industries vocabulary. But strange things started to happen: to arts and culture in the form of George Brandis, and to a seemingly settled world order in the form of Brexit and Trump. Attitudes to the future that presume 'more of the same' now seem unconvincing, yet still we meet people who believe the only way forward is data-driven reports and arguments about 'investment return'. Not only

---

120 Donna Haraway, *Staying with the Trouble: Making Kin in the Chthulucene* (Durham: Duke University Press, 2016), 30.
121 Haraway, *Staying with the Trouble*, 1.

should this change, it *is* changing. It is an irony of history that the high tide of instrumentalism has reached culture just as *homo economicus* is losing ground elsewhere, that affectless rationalising robot who seeks fulfilment as a sovereign consumer and nothing more. It is the time for everyone who cares about arts and culture to get out of the brace position, and come alive to the dialogue about their *inherent* value.

But to do this, and to navigate the crisis, we need perspectives, ideas and words that provide an expansive conversational space. We need to attend to things of longer duration and deeper intensity: to meaning, memory and time. When value is expressed in narratives both practitioners and their publics can avow, it may not be objective universal proof, but it is more than subjective opinion. Statistical analysis without critical understanding only gives us consumer research. And consumer research in culture is a useful servant but a bad master. Focus groups would have scuttled the National Gallery's purchase of *Blue Poles* at the first step.

Until change actually happens, it always seems an unrealistic dream. The most common feelings we have observed in the course of our researches are ones of outrage, frustration, and cynicism. These can contribute to a stance of intellectual defeat that is a greater obstacle to reform than any external oppressive force. For this reason, it is vital to *imagine* an alternative, however imperfect and provisional. The act of contemplating how things *could* be different is the beginning of ensuring that things *are* different. This book seeks to contribute to that process. It does not present another slew of snappy ideas and executive summary cut-throughs in the manner of contemporary 'thought leaders'. It is not in the business of promulgating handy methods and models. It aims to wake us to problems of value, to stimulate the *sense of value* we need to have – do always, in fact, have, in our own hearts and minds – to grace and inform not only our choices in arts and culture, but in the world beyond.

Box 10 In Their Own Words: Artists Talk about Value in the Senate Inquiry

This section contains select quotes from the hundreds of submissions to the 2015 Senate Inquiry into the Brandis arts cuts. It is a sort of word cloud of what matters in Australian arts and culture now. We have chosen the quotes as representative of how people talk when unaffected by bureaucratic protocols and buzzword fads. The Senate Inquiry was a high-stakes situation, where many individuals and organisations were literally arguing for their survival. At this unlooked for and unwarranted moment of stress, the words they spoke sounded to our ears entirely different from the language of 'the funding game'.

We identify quotes only by their submission numbers. Full information, including all 2,719 submissions, can be found at www.aph.gov.au/Parliamentary_Business/Committees/ Senate/Legal_and_Constitutional_Affairs/Arts_Funding/Submissions

'And yet we are told, via the minister, that one of the NPEA guidelines will be "popularity" – popularity with whom? Again, the numbers show us that opera is not so popular, minister. But is it deemed worthy? Apparently yes, and fair enough because great art should be given exposure. But let's take that point further. While we argue that Australians don't value art, it's now becoming apparent through the NPEA that art is indeed valued to the extent that it will now be a privilege to see art, and mainly the privilege of people who can afford the big ticket items and subscriber season tickets.' #677

'We as a nation that so proudly values equality and transparency need to ensure that artists from all levels of the arts sector in all stages of practice have equal access to grants. We as a public have the right for these grant guidelines and outcomes to be transparent. I am concerned that if our artists are forced to go cap in hand to seek funding from private organisations, corporations and companies Australian art will become solely funded, defined and controlled by an elite group that do not necessarily represent the broader diversity and experiences of the Australian society.' #685

'One cannot help but wonder if his withdrawal of support for this model was timed to inflict the most possible distress upon the sector? Everyone is now scrambling to regroup and rethink our futures, if indeed we have one at all … In terms of the ecology of the arts sector, individual artists and youth arts companies are where everything begins. In this new paradigm we are the most fragile, and have everything to lose. Western Sydney young people are the most vulnerable young people in the country. The support of arts programs in this area not only shows that their lives matter, but that their stories and experiences are important and valued in the Australian cultural context.' #242

'When significant arts funding goes, then the making of artworks goes. And finally the artists go. And with them the stories of place, the celebration of Australian life and culture, the chronicling of these times, on this continent. It is an important commodity, and one which I fear would be noticed most tangibly in its retrospective absence.' #248

'The changes proposed by Government to remove funding from the Australia Council for the Arts will adversely affect our ability to continue building a city where culture and art is possible for everyone.' #250

'To think that young musicians, like myself and hundreds of others, won't have access to the same opportunities is a scary prospect. It will result in many young musicians either quitting their trade before their time, or seeking better opportunities overseas. Australia will, as a result, see fewer and fewer world class musicians. And where will that leave the Australian arts community?' #2344

Figure 2: Still from *Song of the Wandering Angus*, based on the WB Teats poem, devised as part of a Masterclass with Eric Bass 2008, photograph by Jeff Busby, puppet by Rachael W Guy, fish puppet by Tim Denton.

'It is currently scarcely viable to operate within the cultural sector as a small company or individual practitioner and I firmly believe that smaller operators generate innovation and diversity. I fear that with the impact of the 2014 and 2015 Commonwealth Budget will be a profound loss of diversity within our cultural "ecosystem" and that we will see the proliferation of a politically driven cultural "monoculture" that does not support or encourage critical enquiry, diversity of opinion or true innovation within the arts.' #2342

'Any suggestion that the NPEA is a potential solution to the problem that excellent Australian art is not being funded is misguided – the problem of "unfunded excellence" has long been recognised by the Australia Council. The solution to the problem of "unfunded excellence" is not to move funding around, but to *increase* the amount of funding available through the Australia Council.' #1168

'She was not always successful and it has taken five years persistence to bring this work to fruition. Five years in which she and I and the creative team have grown as artists together in cross-cultural understanding.' #1167

'As can be deduced, embarking on a career in community music making is not for the ambitious. Practitioners need to have passion and a clear-sighted understanding of the intangible outcomes, as well as the technical musical proficiency required to grow and nurture musical communities. Even though there has been no tangible financial advantage to having chosen a path in music and scholarship, I continue in the field sustained by seeing and understanding what it means to belong to a civil society that values culture in a creative age, even though this is consistently misunderstood, undervalued and misrepresented.' #1166

'We want to continue *KYD*'s contribution to Australia's literary community, support our established writers, and help new Australian voices find their readers. We want to do our bit to ensure Australia has a vibrant, healthy arts culture that not only looks after its artists but sustains the wider public too.' #1165

'All of these areas illustrate a deeper problem that this submission does seek to elucidate, namely that the decision has an impact to a major part of Australian cultural life and the Australian economy and that has been made in such a way as to cause panic, dismay, destabilisation of the sector, loss of productivity, loss of jobs and loss of the development of arts and cultural content.' #342

'Secondly, this pernicious move is directed at the Arts for its perceived opposition to the conservative ideology of the Abbott Government. Senator Brandis' cuts to the Australia Council and the proposed creation of the NPEA is completely impractical and visionless – a hand grenade thrown wilfully into a sector that deserves much more. Confidence is essential to the growth of any industry, and right now the medium-level organisations who support up and coming artists are reeling. Without some certainty they will find it near impossible to invest in emerging, developing and established Australian talent. And all of this as some kind of political, cultural punishment.' #342

'The market does not reward art in a rational manner; that it might is a neo-liberal fantasy that has the same relationship to reality as Hogwarts School of Witchcraft and Wizardry.' #344

'The small to medium sector is home to the life's work of thousands of independent artists.' #466

'Excellence doesn't always mean success. Sometimes it means trying really hard and failing, then trying again, failing a bit more, and getting better.' #467

'Excellence is not determined by location or reputation. A competitive and productive arts environment needs to be subjected to vigorous and searching debate about excellence. Independent, arms-length decision making helps us tackle this debate.' #1131

'I object to these utterly fruitless changes on every level, and I fail to see the reason for this whole shift. The arts are cheap – they generate a significant amount of economic activity for low cost. If a nation as wealthy as Australia decides to go down this path, I feel very sad for our country.' #1479

'George Brandis should be ashamed of himself – taking away funding from the grass roots arts sector. Where does he think the bigger organisations originate??' #1575

'We spend our entire lives WORKING to perfect our craft, so that we can give something to our fellow humans in ways that only art can: it is crucial for our collective emotional and psychological wellbeing.' #1580

'I would have loved to have brought the Australian Ballet to Swan Hill, or even Bell Shakespeare, but the reality is for regional venues like myself, they do not fit.' #2352

'The social, cultural and political ramifications of a Minister determining who has a voice and who is silenced is a profound departure from what we have come to regard as best practice, that being arms-length peer assessment. This move is reflective of an authoritarian approach to cultural and creative diversity and does not serve the shared ideals of a multicultural democratic state.' #1652

'Most importantly – these experiences have a lasting impact on children that is unquantifiable and immeasurable.' #2354

Appendix

GRI and <IR> – Background and Detail, by Fiona Sprott

Founded in Boston in 1997, the Global Reporting Initiative (GRI) grew out of the Coalition for Environmentally Responsible Economies (CERES) and The Tellus Institute, with input from The United Nations Environment Program. GRI has developed a reporting framework for organisations in all sectors of the economy to use as a guide for communicating the impact of their actions on sustainability issues such as climate change, human rights, natural resources, social wellbeing and governance. They state their mission as:

> 'A thriving global community that lifts humanity and enhances the resources on which all life depends'

and

> 'To empower decisions that create social, environmental and economic benefits for everyone.'

The early history of GRI saw the setting up of a multi stakeholder Steering Committee to establish its vision and goals, and expand its scope beyond the core concern of the environment to include social, economic and governance issues. In 1998, GRI developed a Sustainability Reporting Framework which proposed key guidelines for sustainability reporting. In 2002, at the World Summit on Sustainable Development in Johannesburg, GRI launched the second generation of their guidelines for reporting (G2). By this time, GRI was set up as a non-profit organisation in its own right, breaking away from CERES. In 2003, GRI invited a range of organisations to put their name to the mission, and join a Stakeholder Council (SC) with representation from civil, business, financial, governmental and academic sectors.

By 2005, support for GRI and the demand for their reporting framework had grown substantially. Over 3,000 representative experts from a diverse range of sectors contributed to the development of the third generation of the framework (G3). The first global conference on Sustainability and Transparency was held, in Amsterdam, attracting 1,150 participants from 65 countries. GRI went on to enter into formal partnerships with the United Nations Global Compact, and the Organization for Economic Co-operation and Development (OECD). This was the beginning of the next stage of expansion and development to implement their reporting framework practically.

In 2007, GRI moved into educational publication with the release of *Pathways 1*. This was an instructional guide to assist those producing reports of all types. They set up regional offices referred to as Focal Points, beginning with an office in Brazil. They also launched their Application Level Service, which allowed users to self-assess whether their own sustainability reports were meeting required levels of disclosure.

With this suite of programs, partnerships and outlets established, GRI steadily progressed through to its current state of operations. In 2016 GRI launched the inaugural global standards for sustainability reporting (GRI Standards) which enables all organisations to report on their economic, environmental and social impacts and demonstrate how they are actively addressing sustainable development. These standards are considered a trusted reference for policy makers and regulators, available in a modular structure to facilitate easy access to relevant information and to be maintained with updated, current information. The current GRI Standards guidelines adopt clear and simple language to make it easy to understand and use. In 2016 GRI held its 5th Global Conference, with approximately 1,200 leaders in the field of sustainability from 73 countries attending.

Information on GRI and access to the GRI Standards and other publications, databases of information and resources are available at their website: www.globalreporting.org/information/about-gri/gri-history/Pages/GRI's%20history.aspx.

For articles and opinion pieces on the effectiveness of GRI Standards in practice, Environmental Leader publishes extensively on their website: www.environmentalleader.com

Integrated Reporting (<IR>) refers to improvements in integrating the financial and non-financial information contained in an annual report generated by profit and non-profit organisations with official reporting obligations. Commercial firms have obligations to communicate key information on how they are performing financially for the benefit of their shareholders who have invested money and are entitled to a portion of any profits. For non-profit organisations, reporting requirements are geared to funding agreements, donors and managerial oversight structures. A non-profit organisation might want to craft its annual report with the view to attracting new funding, just as a for-profit corporation might want to use it to attract new shareholders. Both types of organisation might use their annual reports as a marketing tool or recruiting tool. The key difference is that shareholders are legally invested in for-profit companies, while stakeholders are not, and are therefore not necessarily entitled to certain information.

Information on the history and development of <IR> can be found at their website: integratedreporting.org

In 2017, the accounting firm Deloitte released 'Annual Report Insights 2017, based on a survey of 100 UK listed companies. They assessed reports against a range of criteria, including the use of alternative performance measures. Compared to 20 years previously where annual reports were on average 43 per cent narrative and 57 per cent financial data, in 2017 narrative sections made up an average of 61 per cent of annual reports. Interestingly Deloitte found that over 60 per cent of the companies focused their attention on communicating the value they created for stakeholders rather than shareholders, and there was an increasing use of KPIs related to employees, customers, and off-balance-sheet resources. Deloitte also highlighted the progress of <IR>.

The report can be viewed or downloaded from their website: www2.deloitte.com/uk/en/pages/audit/articles/annual-report-insights.html

A short time later, another accounting firm, KPMG, published 'The KPMG Survey of Corporate Responsibility Reporting 2017', a survey of 4,900 worldwide companies, including the top 100. This survey also discusses the progress of <IR>, with a specific focus on production of a Corporate Responsibility report, and the addressing of the 17 UN Sustainable Development Goals. Its Executive Summary comments that 'reporting integration is the new normal and "non-financial" is the new financial' and that 'statistics increasingly lack real meaning without information on context and impact'. KPMG argue that the challenge for modern organisations is to go beyond just reporting statistics, and communicate the impact of their activities more comprehensively. In other words, to tell the story of how a company is meeting not only its financial and legal governance requirements, but what impact its actions are having on global sustainability and future value creation. It predicts that more reporting regulation will come into play, and firms can expect that the 'international reporting landscape will continue to be fragmented and dynamic for the foreseeable future'.

The report can be viewed or downloaded from their website: home.kpmg.com/xx/en/home/campaigns/2017/10/survey-of-corporate-responsibility-reporting-2017.html

With the emergence of <IR> and the Integrated International Reporting Council (IIRC), debate has arisen around whether to adopt GRI Standards or <IR> frameworks. Recent literature and commentary have attempted comparison of the various tools and strategies put forward and in 2017 GRI partnered with IIRC to address the range of issues highlighted. The Corporate Leadership group on integrated reporting will investigate how to leverage sustainability reporting within the <IR> framework for best alignment of disclosure.

A quick review of online discussions dedicated to offering advice on improving communication in reporting indicate the following to be important in writing reports:

1. Keep things simple.
2. Use visual material to illustrate the data.
3. Tell a compelling, emotionally engaging story.
4. Think about adaptability of delivery to different audiences. For example, produce one full report for shareholders and/or significant funding agencies, and a microsite on the web for a broader audience with hyperlinks to deeper information if the reader wishes to access it.

The Association of Chartered Certified Accountants (ACCA) released a report in 2017 on analysis of uptake of <IR> in 41 corporate reports sampled from around the world, 'Insights into Integrated Reporting'. They propose the adoption of key changes to improve the effectiveness of integrated reports. See their commentary and recommendations on their findings published on the ACCA website: www.accaglobal.com/an/en/news/2017/april/integrated-reporting.html

Some blogs offer lists of 'imaginative' or 'creative' approaches to annual reports which are good illustrations of the above trends. They provide examples of delivering information in ways that are simplified, visually driven, and communicate the character of what an organisation does more effectively than boilerplate formats. Their examples focus on story, image, and the reader experience. They show modern reports as actively cultivating the understanding of their readership, and engagement with the information presented. Typically, report narratives are clear and sparse, while financial data is highly focused and visually presented

Websites

www.charitywater.org/annual-report/14/#team
resources.oxfam.org.au/pages/preview.php?ref=1692&ext=pdf&k=1820f8
    3246&search=&offset=0&order_by=relevance&sort=DESC&archi
    ve=0&
www.cpaontario.ca/about-cpa-ontario/annual-report
www.kiva.org/about/finances/annualreport/2014
mailchimp.com/2015/#visit-from-a-mariachi-band
www.lemonadeinternational.org/annualreport2013/#frontpage
(good for financial data and stats design in a slideshow format like mail
    chimp use).
www.lemonadeinternational.org/annualreport2013/#frontpage
thankyou.co/built-on-stories/
(nice example of slideshow format with storytelling at heart of presenting
    data).

Bibliography

Arnold, Matthew. *Culture and Anarchy*. Ed. Jane Garnett. Oxford: Oxford University Press, 2006.

Australian Government. *Creative Australia*. National Cultural Policy. Canberra: Australian Government, 2013.

Barnett, Tully. 'The Human Trace in Google Books', in *Border Crossings*, Diana Glenn and Graham Tulloch, eds. Kent Town: Wakefield Press, 2016, pp. 53–71.

——. 'Social Reading: The Kindle's Social Highlighting Function and Emerging Reading Practices.' Australian Humanities Review (2014). www.australianhumanitiesreview.org/archive/Issue-May-2014/barnett.html

Barrett, Lindsay. *The Prime Minister's Christmas Card: Blue Poles and Cultural Politics in the Whitlam Era*. Sydney: Power Publications, 2001.

Becker, Howard. *Art Worlds*. Berkeley: University of California Press, 1982.

Beer, David. *Metric Power*. Basingstoke: Palgrave Macmillan, 2016.

——. 'The Social Power of Algorithms.' *Information, Communication & Society* 20.1 (2017), 1–13.

Belfiore, Eleonora. '"Impact", "Value" and "Bad Economics": Making Sense of the Problem of Value in the Arts and Humanities.' *Arts and Humanities in Higher Education* 14, no. 1 (2015), 95–110.

Belfiore, Eleonora, and Anna Upchurch. *Humanities in the Twenty-First Century: Beyond Utility and Markets*. Basingstoke: Palgrave Macmillan, 2013.

Berlin, Isaiah. *Russian Thinkers*. London: Hogarth Press 1978.

Bishop, Matthew, and Michael Green. *Philanthrocapitalism: How Giving Can Save the World*. New York: Bloomsbury Press, 2008.

Brett, Judith. *The Australian Liberals and the Moral Middle Class: From Alfred Deakin to John Howard*. Melbourne: Cambridge University Press, 2003.

Bridge, Carl. *A Trunk Full of Books: History of the State Library of South Australia and its Forerunners*. Adelaide: Wakefield Press in association with the State Library of South Australia, 1986.

Bookstaber, Richard M. *The End of Theory: Financial Crises, the Failure of Economics, and the Sweep of Human Interaction*. Princeton, NJ: Princeton University Press, 2017.

Boyd, Brian. *On the Origin of Stories: Evolution, Cognition, and Fiction*. Cambridge, Mass: Belknap Press of Harvard University Press, 2009.

Button, James. *Speechless: A Year in My Father's Business*. Carlton, Vic: Melbourne University Press, 2012.

Collini, Stefan. *Speaking of Universities*. London: Verso, 2017.

Darnton, Robert. *The Great Cat Massacre and Other Episodes in French Cultural History*. New York: Vintage Books, 1985.

Davies, William. *The Limits of Neoliberalism*. London: Sage, 2014.

Department of Communications and the Arts. *Creative Nation*. Commonwealth Cultural Policy. Canberra: AGPS, 1994.

Drezner, Daniel. *The Ideas Industry: How Pessimists, Partisans, and Plutocrats Are Transforming the Marketplace of Ideas*. Oxford, New York: Oxford University Press, 2017.

Dutton, Denis. *The Art Instinct: Beauty, Pleasure, & Human Evolution*. New York: Bloomsbury Press, 2009.

Eccles, Robert and Michael Krzus. *One Report: Integrated Reporting for a Sustainable Strategy*. Hoboken, NJ: Wiley & Sons, 2010.

Economist. 'The Birth of Philanthrocapitalism.' *The Economist*, 23 February 2006. www.economist.com/node/5517656.

Florida, Richard L. *The New Urban Crisis: How Our Cities Are Increasing Inequality, Deepening Segregation, and Failing the Middle Class – and What We Can Do about It*. New York: Basic Books, 2017.

Frankfurt, Harry G. *On Bullshit*. Princeton: Princeton University Press, 2005.

Gleeson-White, Jane. *Double Entry: How the Merchants of Venice Shaped the Modern World-and How Their Invention Could Make or Break the Planet*. Sydney: Allen & Unwin, 2011.

——. *Six Capitals: The Revolution Capitalism has to Have or, Can Accountants Save the Planet? Rethinking Capitalism for the Twenty-first Century*. Sydney: Allen & Unwin, 2014.

Goodall, Peter. *High Culture, Popular Culture: The Long Debate*. Sydney: Allen & Unwin, 1995.

Goulder, Naomi. 'Books in Brief: Speaking of Universities by Stefan Collini', 13 October 2017. www.prospectmagazine.co.uk/magazine/books-in-brief-speaking-of-universities-by-stefan-collini.

Haraway, Donna. *Staying with the Trouble: Making Kin in the Chthulucene*. Durham: Duke University Press, 2016.

Harpham, Geoffrey Galt. *The Humanities and the Dream of America*. Chicago: The University of Chicago Press, 2011.

Hughes, Robert. *Culture of Complaint: The Fraying of America*. New York: Oxford University Press, 1993.

Hutter, Michael, and David Throsby, eds. *Beyond Price: Value in Culture, Economics, and the Arts*. Melbourne: Cambridge University Press, 2008.

Industries Assistance Commission. *Assistance to the Performing Arts*. Canberra: AGPS, 1976.

Kahneman, Daniel. *Thinking, Fast and Slow*. London: Allen Lane, 2011.

Lakoff, George, and Mark Johnson. *Metaphors We Live By*. Chicago: University of Chicago Press, 1980.

Lanchester, John. *Whoops! Why Everyone Owes Everyone and No One Can Pay*. London: Penguin, 2010.

Latour, Bruno, and Graham Harman. *Prince and the Wolf: Latour and Harman at the LSE*. London: Zero Books, 2018.

Marr, David. ———. "'So Much of Our Life in It". Arrogant Adelaide and the Theatre of Patrick White'. *Australian Book Review*, May 2012, 12–17.

Mason, Paul. *Postcapitalism: A Guide to Our Future*. London: Allen Lane, 2015.

McMaster, Brian. *Supporting Excellence in the Arts*. London: Department for Culture, Media and Sport, 2008.

Meyrick, Julian. 'Assemblage of Convenience: National Cultural Policy-making 101', *Australian Book Review*, May 2013, 12–14.

———. *Australian Theatre after the New Wave: Policy, Subsidy and the Alternative Artist*. Leiden; Boston: Brill Rodopi, 2017.

———. 'Telling the Story of Culture's Value: Ideal-Type Analysis and Integrated Reporting.' *The Journal of Arts Management, Law, and Society*, 46, no. 4 (7 August 2016), 141–52.

Meyrick, Julian, Richard Maltby, Robert Phiddian, and Tully Barnett. 'Why a Scorecard of Quality in the Arts is a Very Bad Idea'. *The Conversation*, 12 October 2016. theconversation.com/why-a-scorecard-of-quality-in-the-arts-is-a-very-bad-idea-66685

Meyrick, Julian, Robert Phiddian, and Richard Maltby. 'The Mocking of the Modern Mind: Culture and Cartooning in the Age of Je suis Charlie Hebdo'. *Australian Book Review*, April 2015, 47–49.

Meyrick, Julian, and Tully Barnett. 'Culture without "World": Australian Cultural Policy in the Age of Stupid.' *Cultural Trends*, 26, no. 2 (2017), 107–24.

Miévelle, China. *The City and the City*. London: Macmillan, 2009.

Monbiot, George. 'Can You Put a Price on the Beauty of the Natural World? *The Guardian*, 23 March 2018. www.theguardian.com/commentisfree/2014/apr/22/price-natural-world-agenda-ignores-destroys.

Muller, Jerry Z. *The Tyranny of Metrics*. Princeton: Princeton University Press, 2018.

Munslow, Alun. *Narrative and History*. Basingstoke: Palgrave Macmillan, 2007.

Myer, Rupert. 'Arts plus Science Equals Prosperity', Adelaide Advertiser, 28 April 2016. www.adelaidenow.com.au/news/opinion/rupert-myer-arts-and-science-linked-by-innovation-and-creativity/news-story/280003d27694f701279e500d9d519d84.

Noble, Safiya Umoja. *Algorithms of Oppression: How Search Engines Reinforce Racism*. New York: NYU Press, 2018.

Nugent, Helen, & Australian Department of Communications, Information Technology and the Arts. *Securing the Future: Major Performing Arts Inquiry Final Report*. Canberra: Dept of Communications, Information Technology and the Arts, 1999.

O'Neil, Cathy. *Weapons of Math Destruction: How Big Data Increases Inequality and Threatens Democracy.* New York: Crown, 2016.

Patel, Raj. *The Value of Nothing: How to Reshape Market Society and Redefine Democracy.* New York: Picador, 2009.

Phiddian, Robert. 'The Publics of the Adelaide Festival of Ideas.' *University of Toronto Quarterly*, 85, no. 4 (2016), 93–108.

Phiddian, Robert, Julian Meyrick, Tully Barnett, and Richard Maltby. 'Counting Culture to Death: An Australian Perspective on Culture Counts and Quality Metrics.' *Cultural Trends*, 26.2 (2017), 174–80.

Piketty, Thomas and Arthur Goldhammer. *Capital in the Twenty-First Century.* Cambridge Mass.: The Belknap Press of Harvard University Press, 2014.

Plato. *The Republic.* Trans. Henry Lee, 2nd edn rev. Harmondsworth: Penguin, 1987.

Pusey, Michael. *Economic Rationalism in Canberra: A Nation-Building State Changes its Mind.* Melbourne: Cambridge University Press, 2003.

Quiggin, John. *Zombie Economics: How Dead Ideas Still Walk among Us.* Princeton: Princeton University Press, 2010.

Reichmann, W.J. *Use and Abuse of Statistics.* New York: Oxford University Press, 1962.

Rossiter, Ned and Soenke Zehle 'The Aesthetics of Algorithmic Experience', in *The Routledge Companion to Art and Politics*, Randy Martin, ed. London: Routledge, 2015, 214–21.

Rothman, Joshua. 'The Meaning of "Culture".' The New Yorker, 26 December 2014. www.newyorker.com/books/joshua-rothman/meaning-culture.

Schultz, Julianne. 'Australia Must Act Now to Preserve its Culture in the Face of Global Tech Giants.' The Conversation, 2 May 2016. theconversation.com/australia-must-act-now-to-preserve-its-culture-in-the-face-of-global-tech-giants-58724

Seaver, Nick. 'Algorithms as Culture: Some Tactics for the Ethnography of Algorithmic Systems.' *Big Data & Society*, 4.2 (2017), 1–12.

Sessions, David. 'The Rise of the Thought Leader.' The New Republic, 28 June 2017. newrepublic.com/article/143004/rise-thought-leader-how-superrich-funded-new-class-intellectual.

Tal, Eran. 'Old and New Problems in Philosophy of Measurement'. *Philosophy Compass*, 8/12 (2013), 1159–1173.

Throsby, David. 'Perception of Quality in Demand for Theatre' (1982). Reprinted in *Journal of Cultural Economics* (1990): 14/1, 65-82.

Trilling, Lionel. *Beyond Culture: Essays on Literature and Learning.* New York: Viking Press, 1965.

——.'Science, Literature and Culture: A Comment on the Leavis–Snow Controversy.' *Higher Education Quarterly*, 17, no. 1 (1962), 9–32.

Warner, Michael. *Publics and Counterpublics.* New York: Zone Books, 2002.

Watson, Don. *Death Sentence: The Decay of Public Language*. Milsons Point, NSW: Vintage Australia, 2004.

Weber, Max. *The Theory of Social and Economic Organisation*. Trans. and ed. by Talcott Parsons. London: Free Press of Glencoe, 1947.

Wetherell, Sam. 'Richard Florida Is Sorry.' Jacobin, 19 August 2017. jacobinmag.com/2017/08/new-urban-crisis-review-richard-florida.

White, Hayden. 'The Value of Narrativity in the Representation of Reality', *Critical Inquiry*, 7.1 (1980), 5–27.

Williams, Raymond. *Culture and Society, 1780–1950*. Harmondsworth: Penguin, 1993.

——. *Resources of Hope: Culture, Democracy, Socialism*. London: Verso Books, 1989.

Index

Index

About the Authors

Julian Meyrick is a theatre director, historian and cultural policy analyst. He was Associate Director and Literary Adviser at Melbourne Theatre Company, 2002-07, where he established the new play development program, Hard Lines. Currently, he is Strategic Professor of Creative Arts at Flinders University, Artistic Counsel of the State Theatre Company of South Australia, and a member of both Currency House editorial committee and Council of Humanities, Arts and Social Sciences Board. He has directed more than forty award-winning theatre productions, and has written for the Conversation, Daily Review, InDaily, the Monthly and the Sydney Review of Books. His latest book *Australian Theatre after the New Wave* was published by Brill last year.

Dr Tully Barnett is a Lecturer in English at Flinders University, and Research Fellow with the ARC Linkage project Laboratory Adelaide: The Value of Culture. She has 'stuck with the trouble' on digital humanities since multi-path novels on CD were a cool thing and publishes across cultural policy, digital humanities, and reading as a practice. She is the co-author of "Counting culture to death: an Australian perspective on culture counts and quality metrics" (2017). She serves on the boards of the Australasian Association of Digital Humanities and the Australasian Consortium of Humanities Research Centres.

Robert Phiddian is a professor of English at Flinders University. His particular interest is political satire, from Jonathan Swift to John Clarke, and his words appear in media from academic journals and university presses to *Australian Book Review*, the *Conversation* and radio. He was the founding director of the Australasian Consortium of Humanities Research Centres, and has been involved with the Adelaide Festival of Ideas since the event's inception in 1999, thrice chair of the programming committee.

CPSIA information can be obtained
at www.ICGtesting.com
Printed in the USA
FFHW021051041118
49208542-53425FF